Earth Science!
BEST
SCIENCE
PROJECTS

Earth Science Fair Projects

Using Rocks, Minerals, Magnets, Mud, and More

Yael Calhoun

Enslow Publishers, Inc.

40 Industrial Road	PO Box 38
Box 398	Aldershot
Berkeley Heights, NJ 07922	Hants GU12 6BP
USA	UK

http://www.enslow.com

To Alex, Ben Isaac, and Sam—who are teaching me the fine art of asking questions.

Copyright © 2005 by Yael Calhoun

Library of Congress Cataloging-in-Publication Data

Calhoun, Yael.
    Earth science fair projects using rocks, minerals, magnets, mud,
and more / Yael Calhoun.
        p. cm. — (Earth science! best science projects)
    Includes bibliographical references and index.
    ISBN 0-7660-2363-X
    1. Earth science projects—Juvenile literature. I. Title. II. Series.
QE29.C34 2005
550'.7'8—dc22

                                        2004015723

Printed in the United States of America

10 9 8 7 6 5 4 3 2

To Our Readers: We have done our best to make sure all Internet Addresses in this book were active and appropriate when we went to press. However, the author and the publisher have no control over and assume no liability for the material available on those Internet sites or on other Web sites they may link to. Any comments or suggestions can be sent by e-mail to comments@enslow.com or to the address on the back cover.

Illustration Credits: Tom LaBaff

Cover Photo: © 2005 Dynamic Graphics

Contents

Introduction

Before you even left the house this morning, you may have looked at, touched, admired, and eaten materials from the earth. Geology is the study of the earth, from the Latin word *geo* for "earth." One aspect geologists study is the materials that make up the earth. Sometimes people use things directly from the earth, such as granite rocks for building or diamonds for jewelry. People also change the earth's materials, such as refining oil into plastics. In a way, geologists are like earth detectives, using what they know to read the clues of the land to locate earth treasures such as gold, rubies, and oil.

Geologists also study the forces that have shaped the planet, such as erupting volcanoes, moving water and ice, shifting continents, and earthquakes. Scientists still cannot control many of these forces, but they can make more accurate predictions about their occurrences as new scientific equipment is developed.

Geologists also study time. A long time to you may be a year, but to a geologist it is millions, or even billions, of years. Scientists developed the concept of geologic time so that they could think about periods of time since the planet was first formed, which they believe happened 4.6 billion years ago. Geologists study the clues in rocks to try to understand Earth's history. They want to understand not only how the planet was formed, but how it has changed. They also use clues, such as those left in fossils, to try to understand how life has developed. There are still many questions to explore about the earth.

THE SCIENTIFIC METHOD

Science is the process of asking questions about how or why something happens in the natural world. Scientists follow the scientific method to try to find answers. The scientific method begins with a question. The question is reworded as a statement, which is called a hypothesis. Then an experiment is designed to collect information to prove or to disprove the hypothesis. Once the information is collected, the results and conclusions can be reported.

The experiments in this book are designed to help you understand the scientific method. You become a true scientist when you ask your own questions and design an experiment to test them.

The question you might want to answer is: Does water always boil at the same temperature? Your hypothesis, or statement to prove or disprove, could be: Water always boils at the same temperature. Suppose you design an experiment in which you boil water and observe the temperature at which the water boils. An important part of the scientific design is that the experiment be repeatable, which means you or someone else can repeat the experiment and obtain the same or similar results.

The next step is to think about the data you collect and draw your conclusions. Presenting your data in graphs and charts can help you draw conclusions because you can see patterns in your results or areas where you need to collect more data.

Now comes the fun part—you get to ask more questions. Will water boil at that temperature if you heat it slowly? Or quickly? If it has salt in it? If the pot is covered? If you boil it, cool it, and then reboil it? If you begin with ice? If the pot material or the altitude is different? Does the water level in the pot have an effect?

Can you think of some other factors that can change? These factors are called variables. The part that you do not change is called the control. The important thing is to change only one variable at a time so that you know what is responsible for any changing results. For example, if you put salt in the water and cover it at the same time, you will not know which variable caused the change—adding the salt or the cover.

Remember, all experiments are valuable, even if they do not turn out as you expected. You gained some information. Always closely observe what happens. Your observations may prompt you to ask a new question or to change the design of the experiment. A famous example of a scientist who used careful observation is Alexander Fleming. He noticed that bacteria were not growing around the mold in a dish he had forgotten to clean. Instead of calling the experiment a failure, he designed new experiments to study the mold and why bacteria were not growing near it. These observations led to the development of the first antibiotic, penicillin.

The experiments in this book give you a basic design from which you can ask your own questions, changing one variable at a time.

SAFETY FIRST

Keep science fun by following these basic safety rules.

1. Do any experiments or projects, whether from this book or of your own design, under the supervision of a science teacher or other knowledgeable adult.

2. Read all instructions carefully before proceeding with a project. If you have questions, check with your supervisor before going any further.

3. Maintain a serious attitude while conducting experiments. Fooling around can be dangerous to you and to others.

4. Do not eat or drink while experimenting.

5. Do not wash soil, sand, or plaster of Paris (wet or dry) down the sink. It will clog the drain.

6. Wear approved safety goggles when breaking rocks or working with the chemical salol, used for crystal growing.

7. Your science teacher may have chemicals you can use for crystal growing. Be certain to follow all safety

precautions with regard to proper ventilation, contact with your skin and eyes, and disposal of these chemicals.

8. Have a first aid kit nearby while you are experimenting.

9. The liquid in some thermometers is mercury. It is dangerous to touch mercury or to breathe mercury vapor, and such thermometers have been banned in many states. When doing these experiments, use only non-mercury thermometers, such as those filled with alcohol. If you have a mercury thermometer in the house, **ask an adult** if it can be taken to a local mercury thermometer exchange location.

Chapter 1

The Early Planet

Scientists believe that Earth was formed about 4,600 million, which is 4.6 *billion*, years ago. During that time a lot has happened. Our planet cooled to form crusts and oceans. Volcanic steam condensed and added the water and gases necessary to sustain life. About 3.6 billion years ago, bacteria and blue-green algae started to grow. A billion years later, the first large continents formed. The age of ancient life began about 570 million years ago. Humans have been on the planet only about 150,000 years.

Table 1. GEOLOGIC TIME SCALE

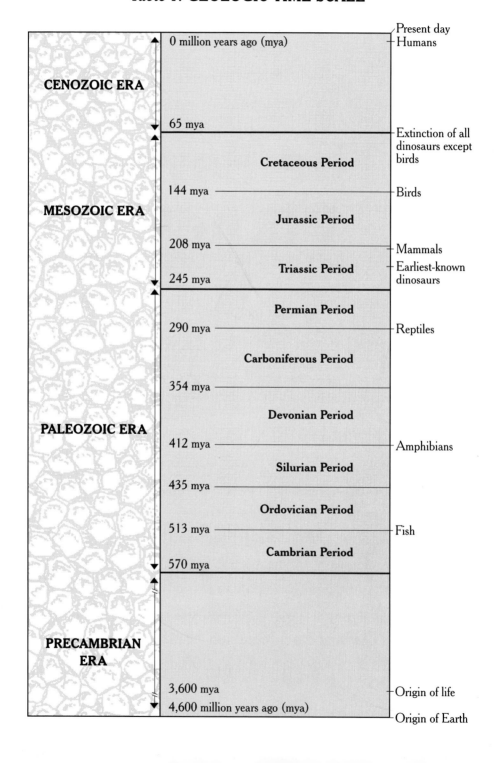

CENOZOIC ERA	0 million years ago (mya)	Present day Humans
	65 mya	Extinction of all dinosaurs except birds
MESOZOIC ERA	**Cretaceous Period**	
	144 mya	Birds
	Jurassic Period	
	208 mya	Mammals
	Triassic Period	Earliest-known dinosaurs
	245 mya	
PALEOZOIC ERA	**Permian Period**	
	290 mya	Reptiles
	Carboniferous Period	
	354 mya	
	Devonian Period	
	412 mya	Amphibians
	Silurian Period	
	435 mya	
	Ordovician Period	
	513 mya	Fish
	Cambrian Period	
	570 mya	
PRECAMBRIAN ERA	3,600 mya	Origin of life
	4,600 million years ago (mya)	Origin of Earth

Scientists who study Earth use a system called the geologic time scale to try to understand how life has developed on our planet. You think about your life or your relative's lives in terms of a few years, maybe even a hundred years. But the geologic time scale begins 4.6 billion years ago. It divides the time into eras and periods (see Table 1). Geologic time is a key part of the study of geology.

Experiment 1.1

Formation of Earth's Layers

Materials

- ✓ measuring spoons
- ✓ salt
- ✓ measuring cups
- ✓ water
- ✓ 1 small jar
- ✓ blue food coloring
- ✓ freezer

- ✓ 1 large glass
- ✓ iron filings (from science or educational supply company)
- ✓ spoon
- ✓ vegetable oil
- ✓ magnet

Next time you take a walk outside, think about the fact that there are layers of very hot, partially melted rocks beneath you. Some rocks are over 2,760°C (5,000°F). But unless you are walking near an active volcano, there is a solid rock layer of almost 100 kilometers (60 miles) between you and the hot rocks.

As the earth was cooling in its early years of formation, layers of rocks with different density settled. Density is a measure of the amount of mass (the amount of matter) in a certain volume (area or space). For example, a soda bottle holding 100 marbles is denser than the same soda bottle filled with 20 marbles. The density is different because although the volume of the soda bottle is the same, the bottle with 100 marbles has more matter in the same volume. Materials that are less dense are lighter and therefore can float on materials that are denser.

The solid outer layer of the earth, called the lithosphere, includes the thin crust and the rigid, top part of the mantle (see Figure 1). Below the lithosphere is the second level of the mantle, called the asthenosphere, where the rocks are denser than those in the outer layer. They are under so much pressure that they are near their melting point. This softness allows the lithosphere above it to slip and slide—much like something sitting on Silly Putty could. The mantle extends halfway to the center of the earth, about 2,900 kilometers (1,800 miles). The earth's center, or core, is the densest layer (see Figure 1c). The core has a radius of about 3,450 kilometers (2,100 miles). It is divided into a liquid outer core and a solid inner core. Scientists believe the core is made of iron and nickel. It is thought that movement in the core's liquid layer generates the earth's magnetic field.

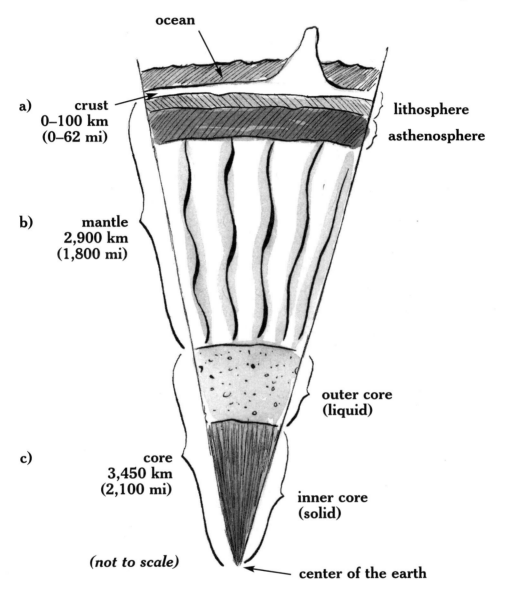

Figure 1.

a) The crust is the rocky layer on the earth's surface. It is thicker under the mountains. b) The mantle is the layer below the crust. c) The innermost layer of the earth is the core.

HOW DOES DENSITY AFFECT LAYER FORMATION?

Make a salt solution by stirring 1 tablespoon of salt into ½ cup of hot tap water in a small jar. Add four drops of blue food coloring. Put the jar in the freezer until the water has frozen into a slush. Add 1 cup of warm (not hot) tap water to a glass. Add ⅛ cup iron filings to the glass and stir. What causes the iron filings to drop to the bottom of the jar? Is iron more or less dense than water? As the earth cooled, the dense materials, most probably iron and nickel, settled to the core.

Slowly add ½ cup of the slushy blue water to the glass by spooning it down the side of the glass. Where does the denser layer settle? This is like the layers of the mantle—the less dense lithosphere settled above the denser asthenosphere as the planet cooled.

Add 2 tablespoons of vegetable oil to the glass. Why does the oil float on the top? The earth's crust, a much lighter silicate rock, is less dense than the mantle below it.

Observe what happens as the water in the glass becomes all one temperature. What would happen if you added cold, blue salt water to warm clear water? Warm salt water to cold, clear water? Draw your conclusions about how density affects the formation of distinct layers.

What happens to the iron filings when you hold a magnet outside the bottom of the jar and move it toward the top? How do you think changes in magnetic fields affect the formation of rock?

Experiment 1.2

Geologic Time

Materials

✓ modeling clay
   (four colors)

✓ black paper

✓ pebbles or small shells

✓ butter knife

✓ science
   notebook

✓ pencil

Geologists use two methods to determine the age of rocks and the earth. One method is called relative geologic age. Geologists have learned that the bottom layers of a rock formation are usually the older rocks. The rock from a volcano that erupted last week sits on top of the rock from an eruption 200 years ago. This method does not give an exact age, but an age relative to the rocks above and below it. Fossils, which are preserved remains, tracks, or imprints from animals or plants that lived at certain times, can also indicate the age of a rock.

The other method, called absolute geologic age, was developed about a hundred years ago when scientists were first able to measure the decay of radioactive elements. Since the elements decay at a known rate, scientists can measure the amount of matter that has decayed in a sample to determine the age of the sample.

Modern geologists use both methods, depending on the kind of rocks for which they are determining the age. Absolute dating, or the exact age, of some rocks can be determined if geologists find the original rock crystals. If the crystals have been changed under heat and pressure, scientists cannot determine when the original crystals formed because the rock now has new crystals. Such rocks must be dated in relation to others, depending upon which layer is on top.

WHAT ARE TWO DIFFERENT METHODS OF DETERMINING THE AGE OF ROCKS?

Press out three layers of different colored clays 2.5 cm (1 in) thick to represent a rock formation. Use one layer as the bottom rock layer (#1), a metamorphic rock. Place a sheet of black paper to represent volcanic ash on top of that. In your science notebook, sketch a diagram of each layer you add. Add another layer of clay (#2) to represent an igneous rock. Could it have been formed before layer #1? Why? On top of layer #2, press a layer of pebbles or shells to represent fossils in an ancient ocean. Add the last layer of clay, #3 (see Figure 2), to represent a sedimentary rock. Now which layer is the youngest (which layer formed last)? This is relative dating—one layer in relation or relative to the other.

Volcanic ash contains original rock crystals, so that layer can be used for determining absolute geologic time. Is layer #1 (the bottom layer) older or younger than the layer of volcanic ash? If you knew the exact time the ash layer was formed, would you say that layer #1 happened before or after that time? That is relative time.

With a butter knife, cut off a 5-cm (2-in) slab of the clay formation and place it on its side. As a geologist, you have already determined the age of the larger layers. How could you determine the age of these tilted layers if they were found in a different location? (Hint: Besides the ash layer, what other clues could be held in these rocks? Would you look for fossils?)

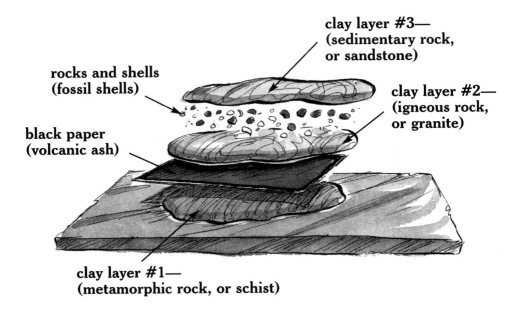

clay layer #3—
(sedimentary rock,
or sandstone)

rocks and shells
(fossil shells)

clay layer #2—
(igneous rock,
or granite)

black paper
(volcanic ash)

clay layer #1—
(metamorphic rock, or schist)

Figure 2.

To understand how fossils are formed in layers of rock, press a sheet of black paper over a layer of clay. Add another layer of clay and press a layer of shells or pebbles over this. Add a final layer of clay.

What happens if you cut the layers in half, lifted one side up 8 cm (3 in), and pushed a fourth color of clay under it? This represents an intrusion caused by cooling magma. Where is the youngest rock now? Can you make a map of this cross-section?

Science Project Idea

People try to understand geologic time by comparing it to something they know. For example, using a 24-hour day, if the first hour were the formation of the planet, and the last minutes were the time humans have been on Earth, at what hour is the age of dinosaurs? Can you relate geo-logic time in the same way to the months of a year? To folds in a paper fan? How could you use sand or salt grains or water drops? (Hint: If your life represents 2.5 ml (1/2 tsp), how much is equal to the age of dinosaurs?) How about using the seats in a large stadium (say, for 80,000 people)? Make a display of your comparisons.

Experiment 1.3

Under What Conditions Will Fossils Form?

Materials

✓ 2 glass jars

✓ labels

✓ garden soil or compost (potting soil will not work because it has no microorganisms)

✓ markers

✓ ruler

✓ 2 lettuce leaves

✓ water

✓ sand

Note: This process takes 3 to 4 weeks.

Fossils are remains or traces of plants and animals from prehistoric times. They can take many forms, from pollen grains to animal tracks to *T. rex* skeletons. Scientists can learn about past climates, ages of rocks, and extinctions from studying fossils. For example, certain corals living today can only be found in warm waters. If scientists find these corals in prehistoric rocks, they know the climate at that time was warm. Sometimes whole species, or groups, of animals suddenly stop appearing in fossils. That could mean a great extinction occurred.

Most plants and animals do not leave fossils. They just decompose. But sometimes the hard parts of organisms, such as bones, are preserved in fossils. Fossil bones form when silica and calcite crystals dissolved in water gradually replace the bone with rock crystals. Other types of fossils are simply imprints, or molds, of the plant or animal. Sometimes the imprint fills with sediment and hardens, forming a cast.

Rarely, the whole animal becomes a fossil. Insects were trapped in the hardened resin (amber) of ancient trees. Woolly mammoth skeletons have been found frozen in arctic tundra, and a mummified sloth was preserved in a dry cave of Nevada.

WHAT ENVIRONMENTAL CONDITIONS ARE NECESSARY FOR FOSSILS TO FORM?

Label two glass jars as JAR #1 and JAR #2. Fill each jar with 5 cm (2 in) of garden soil or compost. Place a lettuce leaf on top of the soil in each jar. Then add 8 cm (3 in) of soil on top of each lettuce leaf. Slowly add water to Jar #1 so that it is three quarters full (see Figure 3). Leave the jars on a counter (but not in direct sunlight) for three weeks. After three weeks, empty the jars and compare the condition of the lettuce leaves. Did the leaves in Jar #2 decompose more than in Jar #1? In which jar is there more oxygen present to allow decomposition to occur?

Repeat the experiment using damp garden soil and dry sand. Vary the conditions (wet and hot, cold and dry, cold and wet). What environmental conditions are better for preserving fossils? (Hint: If the environmental conditions decompose

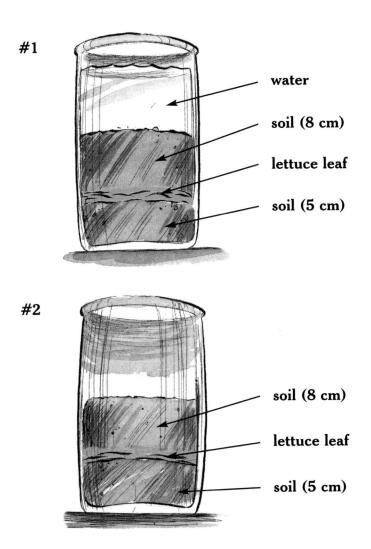

Figure 3.

To understand why fossils are preserved only under certain environmental conditions, put garden soil into two jars. Place a lettuce leaf on the soil in each jar, then add another layer of soil to each jar. Add water to Jar #1 and wait three weeks to see what happens to the leaves.

leaves, what else would get decomposed?) Where would these conditions occur in nature? Why are many fossils found in ancient ocean beds?

Science Project Idea

There are some areas in which fossils are abundant. Create a map of the world or of your region of the country showing what fossils have been found there. This is especially interesting to do with dinosaur fossils. Include information about the geology of the area or about past environmental conditions that shows why fossils were preserved. (For example, note whether the area was once a great inland ocean or lake.) Would you expect to find fossils in a tropical rain forest?

Experiment 1.4

Continental Drift and Fossil Clues

Materials

✓ world map—Africa should be about 8 cm (3 in) long	✓ rolling pin
	✓ tracing paper and pencil
	✓ scissors
✓ mixing bowl	✓ butter knife
✓ measuring cups	✓ waxed paper
✓ flour	✓ leaf
✓ water	✓ rock
✓ fork or spoon	✓ ruler or tape measure

Looking at a map of the world, you can see how the west coast of Africa and the east coast of South America could fit together. In fact, scientists believe that over 200 million years ago, all of the continents were one big landmass. They call it Pangaea, from the Greek words for "all" (*pan*) and "earth" (*gaia*). Scientists deduced this by tracking the paths of old glaciers, studying ancient magnetic fields, and matching rock formations and fossils.

In 1910, an American geologist named Frank Taylor proposed that the continents actually move. He based his idea on data that tracked the paths of old glaciers. In 1912, a German scientist named Alfred Wegener studied fossils, rock formations, and the directions of glacial striations (marks on rocks) to develop his theory about Pangaea. He thought that only the continents moved and called the theory continental drift.

Few people believed these ideas until the 1960s, when scientists had the equipment to refine the ideas into a theory known as plate tectonics. Scientists now understand that the outer layer of the earth is composed of 12 large plates and several smaller ones. These plates lie under both the ocean and the continents. They all fit together like a giant puzzle, but unlike a puzzle, the pieces move (or drift) because of heat and pressure from below.

HOW DO FOSSILS AND GLACIERS LEAVE CLUES ABOUT CONTINENTAL MOVEMENT?

In a mixing bowl, mix 1 cup of flour with ½ cup of water to make dough. Roll it out to cookie dough thickness (¼ in). Use tracing paper and a pencil to trace the shapes of Africa and South America from a map (Africa should be about 8 cm, or 3 in, long). Cut out the shapes, place them on top of the dough, and cut along the edges with a butter knife. Place them on a small piece of waxed paper so that South America is under the overhang in Africa. Press a leaf across the two continents to make a fossil imprint. Remove the leaf. Press and drag a small rock (which represents a glacier) from the southern coast of Africa across the matching coast of South America.

Take one 46-cm (18-in) piece of waxed paper and make five 2.5-cm (1-in) pleated folds in it, like a paper fan (see Figure 4) and press them flat. Now place the two continents, sides touching, lengthwise (north to south) on the pleats. Slowly pull the ends of the waxed paper apart. The continents are now separated by an area of waxed paper; this area represents the Atlantic Ocean. What happened to the fossil imprint and the glacier marks? If the fossil of a certain animal is found only on the west coast of Africa and the east coast of South America, is it reasonable to think that the continents were once closer?

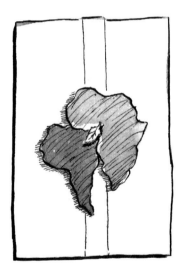 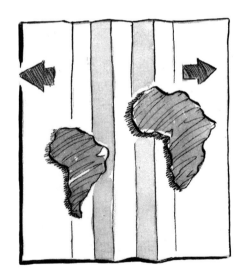

Figure 4.

To help you understand continental drift, fold some waxed paper into pleats like a fan. Press the folds flat. Place the cutout continents on the folds. Pull the waxed paper out from each side.

Try to make all seven continents and align them on the pleated wax paper so that there are no gaps between them. Before pulling the waxed paper apart, leave clues that could be used to track the movement of the continents: fossils, magnetic fields of rocks that were formed at the same time, and specific rock formations. What other clues could be used?

Science Project Idea

In one hundred years, New York and Spain will be about 2.4 m (8 ft) farther apart than they are now. Research how scientists think the continents will be aligned in 100 million years. (Hint: What will happen in the Red Sea? In Africa?) Create several maps to show the movement of the continents over time.

Experiment 1.5

Plate Tectonics

Materials

✓ maps of geology and topography of your city or state (available at sporting goods stores, city hall planning offices, or online; see appendix)

✓ paper

✓ colored pencils

✓ camera

✓ library or the Internet

The earth's crust and the top part of the mantle are made of solid rocks. This layer is cracked, like the broken shell of a hard-boiled egg. The pieces are called plates. Because plates rest on a layer of rocks that are partially melted, they move. In the theory of plate tectonics, it is not just the continents that are drifting, but also the plates to which they may be attached. The energy that causes the plates to move comes from the heat and pressure deep within the earth. The mantle rock is heated unevenly, causing the asthenosphere to move in a swirling motion.

Plates move in several ways. At the bottom of the Atlantic Ocean, hot, melted rock beneath the earth's surface, called magma, pushes through the crust and spreads the plates apart. This action forms the longest mountain chain on the planet, the Mid-Atlantic Ridge. The ridge extends south from about 55 degrees North in the North Atlantic, then branches in the South Atlantic into the Indian and Pacific Oceans.

A second way plates can move is when the denser, heavier ocean crust slides under the lighter crust of the continents, as around the Pacific Ocean plates. The action, called subduction, can lift the continents to form mountains, cause powerful earthquakes, and build volcanoes. Plates can also collide or slide past each other. This can also cause earthquakes and build mountains.

HOW HAS PLATE MOVEMENT AFFECTED THE LAND WHERE YOU LIVE?

Visit USGS (United States Geological Survey) offices, your state Geological Survey, NRCS (Natural Resources Conservation Service) offices, or city planning offices to find maps on the geology and topography (the land surface) of your area. Locate the features you know. Use these maps to create your own map of topographic features in your area that are a result of plate movement (for example: earthquake faults, large rock outcroppings, volcanoes, mountains, or canyons). Take photographs of as many features as you can.

Research the history of the features by contacting geologists who work for the state or federal government or a university. For example, when was the earthquake fault last active? What records are kept on earthquake activity in the area? Is any earthquake activity predicted in your lifetime? Are the mountains growing or eroding? What is causing this? How old are the rocks in the canyon? Is there evidence of rock uplifting? For example, can you see areas in which the layers are tilted?

What is the name of the tectonic plate on which you live? Where is the nearest other large plate? Are the two plates colliding or pulling apart? If the plates moved differently, what might change about the topography where you live? Your map could include your city, your state, or your region of the country.

Science Project Idea

Do the same research as in Experiment 1.5, but choose a place in the world about which you would like to learn or that you would like to visit. For example, explore Old Faithful and other geysers in Yellowstone National Park, the Himalayas, Mount St. Helens, or some Hawaiian volcanoes. Create a map of the plates that have created the landforms. Are the features (mountains, volcanoes, geysers) becoming more active or growing? Why? Where are similar features found in the world? Where might they be found in the future, given the current direction of plate movement?

Chapter 2

To Build a Planet

Our planet is subject to many forces of change. Some changes are slow and hard to see, such as when pressure causes a mountain to grow several centimeters a year. Others are explosive and dramatic, such as when volcanoes create islands or bury cities.

Many of the changes that have been building our planet occur because there are gases and thick layers of hot, partially melted rocks below the earth's surface that exert pressure on the plates in this solid rocky outer layer. These plates move over the less rigid asthenosphere. But plate movement is not always smooth. Plates can collide and push each other up, stretch out and break, or dive under each other. The movement can cause earthquakes, volcanoes, tidal waves, and mountain building.

From the earliest times, humans have tried to explain the changes in the earth. Aristotle, a Greek philosopher who lived about 2,400 years ago, believed that wind escaping from caves caused earthquakes. According to some traditional American Indian beliefs, the earth sat on a giant turtle, and the earth rocked when the turtle moved. Modern scientists use new technologies to understand and predict earthquake and volcano activity.

The experiments in this chapter will help you understand how these forces are building our planet.

Experiment 2.1

Earthquakes and the Stability of Building Foundations

Materials

- ✓ 8 drinking straws
- ✓ ruler
- ✓ marking pen
- ✓ 1 piece of thick card-board about 50 cm (20 in) square
- ✓ measuring cup
- ✓ sand
- ✓ mud
- ✓ salt
- ✓ pebbles
- ✓ 12 Styrofoam blocks about 8 cm (3 in) square
- ✓ paper clips
- ✓ science notebook
- ✓ pencil

An earthquake is the sudden release of energy from the earth. Most earthquakes happen along the edges of plates. The plates slip, slide, and crash against each other, releasing energy. About 80 percent of all earthquakes happen around the edge of the Pacific Ocean, because the ocean plates there are collid-ing with the continental plates.

Scientists have been recording earthquakes for centuries. They use a seismograph, an instrument that detects and mea-sures the vibrations from an earthquake. Earthquakes generate three kinds of waves: P-waves, S waves, and surface waves. P-waves (pressure waves) move by a pushing/pulling motion, like compression waves on a spring or Slinky toy, and travel the fastest. P-waves can travel through solids, liquids, and gases (see Figure 5a). S waves (secondary waves) vibrate from side to side, or shake (see Figure 5b). S waves travel only through solid materials, so they move more slowly than P-waves. When P-waves and S waves reach the surface, they cause the third type of seismic waves, called surface waves (see Figure 5c). These travel on the top of the ground and can move like ocean waves. They can also move side to side. These are the waves that make buildings and bridges collapse.

Scientists use the Richter scale to measure the amount of energy an earthquake releases. The largest magnitude ever recorded was 8.9, and the smallest we can feel is 2. Each whole-number increase on this scale means that 31 times more energy was released.

ARE SOME BUILDING FOUNDATIONS MORE STABLE THAN OTHERS?

Arrange 8 drinking straws about 3 cm (1 in) apart on a table. With a marker and a ruler, divide a piece of thick cardboard (about 50 cm, or 20 in, square) into four sections (see Figure 6). Place the cardboard on top of the straws. Place ½ cup of dry sand in one section, ½ cup of mud in one section, ½ cup of salt in one section, and ½ cup of pebbles in another

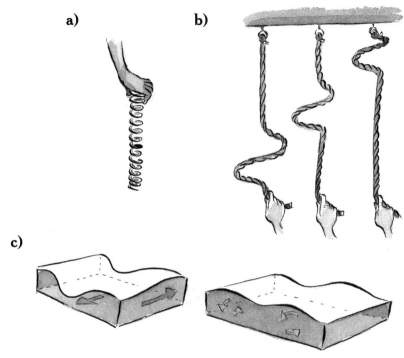

Figure 5.

a) P-waves act like the push and pull action of a spring.
b) S waves move only through solid particles. They are side-to-side or up-and-down disturbances. c) Surface waves are complex. They can travel side to side and up and down like an ocean wave.

so that each pile is at least 2.5 cm (1 in) high. Now construct four identical buildings. For each one, stack 3 Styrofoam blocks and push a straightened paper clip down the center to connect them. Place a building on each of the four piles, pressing it down slightly so that there is a flat foundation on top of the pile.

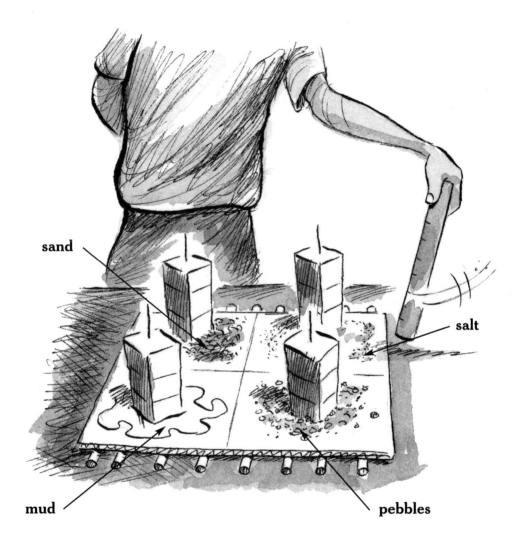

Figure 6.

Which type of foundation best absorbs seismic vibrations? To find out, place a pile of foundation material in each square or a piece of cardboard resting on straws. Press a building into the material. Tap the cardboard to create "seismic waves."

Create a table like Table 2 in your science notebook. Record the order in which your buildings fall when you tap the cardboard lightly with the ruler.

Table 2.

STABILITY OF DIFFERENT FOUNDATIONS

Order in Which Buildings Fall			
	1st Trial	2nd Trial	3rd Trial
Dry Sand			
Mud			
Salt			
Pebbles			

Continue tapping the cardboard with the ruler until all the buildings have fallen. Do the experiment three times. Does the type of foundation affect a building's resistance to earthquakes? Who would benefit from such information?

Does it matter which corner of the cardboard you tap? What effect does the building shape have (dome, cone, pyramid, or top-heavy skyscraper)? Try the same experiment using different bridge designs. What happens when other materials are used as a foundation?

Science Project Idea

Collect information on earthquakes by contacting the USGS (United States Geological Survey), your state Geological Survey office, your zoning inspector's office at city hall, or a university geology department in your area. What types of maps are available (satellite images, geologic maps)? What is the earthquake history of your area, and what are the predictions? Does your city have any earthquake zoning regulations or building codes concerning city buildings or bridges? Looking at a map of earthquake activity in the United States, what cities do you think should have strong earthquake building codes? Do they?

Experiment 2.2

The Forces That Create Volcanoes

Materials

- ✓ balloon that fits snugly onto a straw
- ✓ straw
- ✓ glass bowl or casserole dish
- ✓ scissors
- ✓ 2 Styrofoam plates
- ✓ water
- ✓ red food coloring
- ✓ small stone (optional)
- ✓ ruler
- ✓ vegetable oil
- ✓ glue
- ✓ tissue

Volcanoes form when molten rock breaks through the earth's surface. Rocks under the earth's surface can be melted into magma. The magma collects in a chamber below the earth's crust until it is pushed to the earth's surface.

One cause of volcanoes is when the denser rocks of the ocean plates sink under the lighter, less dense continental plates. The molten rock beneath the surface is pushed up as a volcano. Mount St. Helens in the northwestern United States is an example of a volcano formed under these conditions. The entire area around the Pacific Ocean is an active site for volcanoes as the ocean plates sink under the continental plates. This has created what is called the Ring of Fire, referring to the many active volcano sites.

Volcanoes also form when there are breaks in the ocean floor. This is called seafloor spreading. Seafloor spreading happens when magma moves to the surface and pushes the lithosphere apart.

A third way volcanoes form is when magma comes through a thin spot in the earth's crust. The crust over the magma is stretched thin by plate movement, which allows magma to penetrate through the crust. This creates hot spot volcanoes. The islands of Hawaii were formed by hot spot volcanoes.

WHAT ARE SOME FORCES THAT CREATE VOLCANOES?

Stretch a balloon several times. Stretch its neck over a straw, and make sure you can inflate the balloon. Then let the air out. With the straw still in the end of the balloon, place the balloon along the bottom of a glass bowl or casserole dish. Using scissors, carefully trim a Styrofoam plate so it just fits into the top of the bowl, cutting an opening at the edge to insert the straw. Remove the plate from the bowl. Fill the bowl ¾ full of water and add 10 drops of red food coloring. This represents magma. If the balloon floats, place a small stone on it to keep it down. Add 1 cm (½ in) of vegetable oil to the bowl. The oil represents the zone of partially melted rock in the asthenosphere. Cut the plate into three pieces, and fit the pieces back together like a puzzle on top of the oil (see Figure 7a). These pieces represent the plates on the earth's surface.

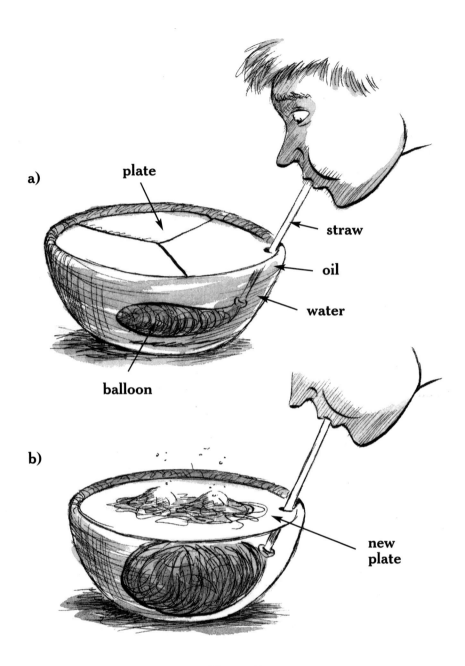

Figure 7.

A MODEL OF MAGMA RISING TO THE EARTH'S SURFACE

a) What happens when you gently blow into the straw to expand the balloon? b) See how magma presses through thin spots in the earth's plates.

Make sure the straw is sticking through the notch so that you can blow up the balloon.

Why is there no movement of magma (red water) or partially melted rock (the oil) at this time? Now gently blow into the straw so that the balloon expands. This represents the pressure from heat and gas generated from within the earth. What happens? What happens when you increase the force (pressure) of your breath into the balloon?

Set up the experiment again, but instead of cutting a Styrofoam plate into puzzle pieces, cut two 2.5-cm- (1-in-) diameter circles in a new plate and glue the edges of a piece of tissue around the holes (see Figure 7b). The tissue represents thin spots in the crust. What happens when you blow into the balloon?

What are the volcanic predictions for Yellowstone National Park?

Experiment 2.3

Mountain-Building Forces

Materials

- ✓ flour
- ✓ measuring cups
- ✓ water
- ✓ mixing bowl
- ✓ rolling pin
- ✓ waxed paper
- ✓ ruler
- ✓ yellow modeling clay
- ✓ marbles, shells, paper clips, pebbles (or other small objects)
- ✓ tablespoon
- ✓ cooking oil
- ✓ soil (any kind)
- ✓ butter knife
- ✓ notebook
- ✓ pencil

When you look at a mountain, you cannot see the complex geological process that took millions of years to create it. In fact, before scientists understood plate tectonics, it was thought that mountains formed as the new earth's crust cooled, shrank, and shriveled.

Today we know that most mountains are built as one plate shoves against or under another. Sometimes two continental plates collide, and land is crunched. This is how many of the major mountain chains in the world have formed, including the Urals, the Alps, the Appalachians, and the Himalayas.

When mountains are formed, portions of the earth get moved around. Rocks and minerals, including gold and diamonds, can be pushed toward the surface. Layers of rocks that were once flat can be pushed so they point toward the sky. Fossils from ancient oceans can be pushed to the top of a mountain.

HOW DOES THE PROCESS OF MOUNTAIN FORMATION EXPOSE NEW LAYERS OF EARTH?

Make some dough by mixing 8 cups of flour with 4 cups of water in a bowl. Roll half of the dough onto a 2-ft piece of waxed paper until it is about the size of an 8 $\frac{1}{2}$ x 11-in piece of paper, and about 5 cm (2 in) thick. Roll out a tube of yellow clay that is about 20 cm (8 in) long and 2.5 cm (1 in) thick. This represents a vein of gold. Press it across the middle of the white dough. Now press some marbles, paper clips, pebbles, and shells (or whatever small objects you have collected) onto the surface of the white dough (See Figure 8a). These are the fossils, silver deposits, and other hidden earth treasures. Make a small well with your finger and add 1 tablespoon of cooking oil. This represents an oil deposit. Roll out the other piece of white dough to the same thickness as the first, and place it over the top. Spread a small layer of soil on the top. At this stage, before the process of mountain building, how many fossils and minerals are exposed?

With a butter knife, cut the layers in half. You now have two continental plates (see Figure 8b). Place your hands on either end of the waxed paper and slowly slide them toward the center. Your hands are pressing the continental plates together.

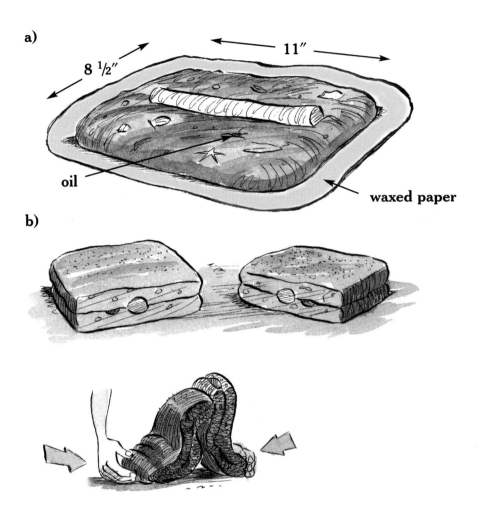

Figure 8.

a) To understand how oil, minerals, and fossils move from under the earth's surface to become exposed on the top, create layers of hidden treasures. b) To create the effect of the earth's plates being pushed together as mountains are formed, cut the dough in half and slowly push the waxed paper together.

What happens? Continue to push the sides together until you have made a mountain range. Record the number of diamonds (marbles), fossils (shells), veins of gold (yellow dough) or silver (paper clips), or oil wells that are exposed after the uplift.

Why can fossils of ancient sea creatures be found on the tops of mountains? How else can you change the mountains or expose more of the treasures? (Hint: Press the dough down again so that all the treasures are covered and use a butter knife to cut the dough in half again, then move the pieces of the plates in different ways.)

Chapter 3

Earth's Materials

R ocks, minerals, and soil are important in more ways than most people can list. Minerals are in toothpaste, televisions, magazine paper, plastics, clothing and rug fibers, breakfast cereal, drywall and plaster walls, jewelry, and bathroom tiles. In fact, people make thousands of products from over 2,500 different kinds of minerals on the planet. Rocks give us a lot of support. Buildings, bridges, and roads are only a few uses we have for rocks. Sometimes we just like to look at rocks—small rocks, like diamonds, and larger rocks, like those in the Grand Canyon.

Minerals and rocks are interesting not only because of what we do with them, but also because of where they have been. All rocks are classified into three categories: igneous, sedimentary, or metamorphic. Each type of rock has its own story, according to how it formed and how it has changed over time.

Different soils behave differently, just like people. Some are hard to work with, some do not change much, some take off with the slightest change in weather, and some are old and actually called senile.

Experiment 3.1

Minerals and How They Form

Materials

✓ **an adult**
✓ powdered alum (2.75 oz from grocery store)
✓ 3 clear glass jars
✓ spoon
✓ water
✓ pot
✓ stove
✓ shallow plate
✓ measuring cups and spoons
✓ ruler
✓ thread
✓ 2 pencils
✓ waxed paper
✓ clock or watch with second hand
✓ notebook
✓ pencil

Note: It takes about 3 weeks to grow a large crystal.

There are three things to know about what makes a mineral. First, minerals are made from materials in the earth's crust called elements. Elements are the basic building blocks of everything on earth. Silicon, oxygen, and calcium are common elements. Second, minerals have a unique chemical makeup. This means that each mineral is made of certain elements and no others. And third, minerals occur in a crystal structure that is unique for each. A crystal structure is an orderly, repeating pattern or arrangement of molecules, like frozen water in a snowflake. Salt has a repeating pattern of sodium and chloride molecules in a cubic structure.

It takes just the right combination of available elements, time, space, and temperature to grow a large crystal, and that doesn't happen very often in nature. If a crystal is subjected to heat or pressure (or both) over time, it will reorganize into a new crystal structure.

HOW DO CRYSTALS GROW?

You can grow a crystal in one of the ways that crystals grow in nature. To make a crystal-forming (supersaturated) solution, **have an adult** slowly stir about $1/3$ cup of powdered alum into $1/2$ cup of boiled water in a clear glass jar until some solids settle to the bottom. Put 2 tablespoons of the solution on a shallow plate. Let the plate sit for two days until you see several "seed" crystals about 0.5 cm ($1/4$ in) long. Save the remainder of the solution in the jar.

Label two other glass jars as JAR #1 and JAR #2. **Have an adult** put ½ cup of boiled water into Jar #1 and stir about ⅓ cup of alum into it until some solids settle to the bottom. Add the remainder of the alum solution you made before to Jar #1 and stir. Let the solution cool. Fill Jar #2 with cool tap water.

Select two crystals that have formed on the plate. Tie one end of a 13-cm (5-in) thread around each crystal. Tie the other end around a pencil and suspend one crystal in each jar so that it is covered in water (see Figure 9).

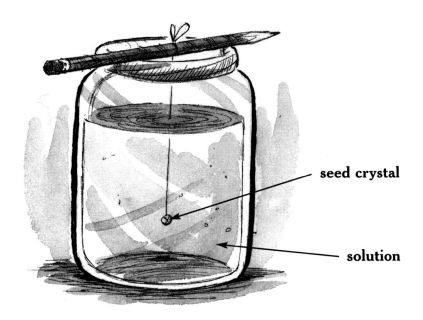

seed crystal

solution

Figure 9.

To grow a large crystal, tie a thread around a seed crystal. Tie a pencil to the other end and suspend the crystal in a super-saturated solution. Cover Jar #1 with waxed paper and leave for several weeks.

Observe the crystals for two minutes. What happens? Why did the seed crystal in jar #2 dissolve? Cover Jar #1 with waxed paper and let it sit for several weeks. What happens? (If the crystal in Jar #1 dissolves or does not grow, it means your alum solution was not supersaturated. Try again.) Record your results. What conditions are required for a crystal to grow?

How could you grow an even larger crystal in Jar #1? What would happen if you put the crystal in a new supersaturated, cooled alum solution (with no competing crystals in the jar) every few days? What would happen if you shook the jar every day? If you kept the water cold or heated it? If you let dust settle in the water? If you used nylon instead of cotton thread? In nature, where would you expect to find large crystals?

Science Project Idea

Note: Salol is not a hazardous compound, but you should wear safety goggles while using it. Do not dump the chemical down the sink.

Crystals can take many years to form in nature, but you can watch some crystals form quickly. Put a tightly capped glass bottle with some salol (phenyl salicylate) in a bowl of hot tap water and watch the salol melt. Remove the bottle from the bowl of hot water. Watch as it cools to room temperature. What forms? If you vary the cooling rate by putting the bottle in ice water, what happens?

Put melted salol solution on glass slides of different temperatures. Do the crystals form at the same rate on hot and cold slides? Why are the crystals different sizes?

Experiment 3.2

Identifying Minerals

Materials

- ✓ **an adult**
- ✓ at least five mineral samples (these can be purchased from a rock shop or over the Internet)
- ✓ water
- ✓ towel
- ✓ hammer
- ✓ penny
- ✓ butter knife
- ✓ steel file
- ✓ porcelain tile
- ✓ field guide to minerals
- ✓ science notebook
- ✓ pencil

People have developed thousands of uses for minerals, from using mineral crystals in computers to decorating their fingers with jewelry. Geologists also identify minerals to give us clues about how the earth formed.

A mineral is a repeating pattern of certain elements in a crystalline form. Quartz, for example, is a mineral that is always formed from crystals made from the elements silicon and oxygen. Geologists have identified certain characteristics of minerals to identify them. You can obtain a lot of valuable information just by looking at the mineral: What color is it? Is it shiny? Does it have flat surfaces? Other mineral characteristics include its hardness and the color of the streak it leaves when it is rubbed across a porcelain tile.

There are additional laboratory tests that involve heat and chemicals. But many minerals can be identified using such simple tools as a magnifying glass, a penny, a steel file, and a field guide to minerals.

HOW CAN YOU IDENTIFY MINERALS?

Examine at least five mineral samples and record the information you collect. In your science notebook, make a chart like Table 3.

Table 3.

CHARACTERISTICS OF MINERALS

Characteristics of Minerals						
Color	Hardness	Cleavage	Streak	Luster	Other	Mineral Name

First, record the color of each mineral you find or purchase. Although mineral color can vary greatly, it is still an important first clue. Look at the mineral wet. **Have an adult** wrap it in a towel and break it with a hammer; sometimes the outside of the mineral is quite weathered and the color is hard to see.

A second clue is the mineral's hardness. You can determine hardness by scratching each mineral with your fingernail, a penny, a butter knife, and a steel file. If a mineral can be scratched with a fingernail, the hardness is 2.5; with a penny, hardness is 3; a butter knife blade, hardness is 5.5; and with a steel file, the hardness is about 7.5. Look at the Mohs' Scale of

Hardness (Table 4) to compare your results to the hardness ranking of the ten minerals in this scale. This is a relative scale, meaning minerals are being compared to each other or to something else. Sometimes the numbers are in-between. For example, a mineral that scratches calcite but not fluorite is rated as having a hardness of 3.5.

Table 4.
SCALE OF MINERAL HARDNESS (MOHS' SCALE)

Hardness Number	Mineral
1	Talc
2	Gypsum[a]
3	Calcite[b]
4	Fluorite
5	Apatite[c]
6	Orthoclase[d]
7	Quartz
8	Topaz
9	Corundum
10	Diamond

Can be scratched with a [a]fingernail, [b]penny, [c]glass, [d]steel file.

Cleavage, or the ability of the mineral to break off into flat surfaces or planes, is also used to identify minerals. To determine if the mineral has cleavage, look at how the mineral broke with the hammer. If it showed flat surfaces (as with calcite and halite) or you could peel it off in sheets (as with mica), then it has cleavage.

Next, rub the mineral across a porcelain tile and record the color of the streak. Is it red, white, gray, or black? Does it leave a streak? Another clue is called luster, which is divided into metallic (looking like a metal) or nonmetallic (not looking like a metal). Nonmetallic luster includes such descriptions as glassy, greasy, silky, and pearly.

These mineral characteristics are given in field guides to minerals, so you can now try to complete the last column of the chart in your notebook by identifying each mineral. Read in the field guide about how the mineral was formed. In what rocks is the mineral found? Where is the mineral commonly found in the United States (or the world)? For what is the mineral used?

Science Project Idea

Some minerals are fluorescent or phosphorescent, or glow with a light from electromagnetic radiation. There are hundreds of minerals that have these properties. Calcite is one common example. Design some experiments using both short-wave and long-wave ultraviolet lights to demonstrate how different minerals fluoresce or phosphoresce.

Experiment 3.3

How Igneous Rocks Are Formed

Materials

- ✓ **an adult**
- ✓ measuring cup
- ✓ powdered alum (2.75 oz from grocery store)
- ✓ spoon
- ✓ water
- ✓ pot
- ✓ stove
- ✓ oven mitt
- ✓ glass jar
- ✓ 2 glass pie plates
- ✓ freezer
- ✓ magnifying glass
- ✓ ruler
- ✓ sugar
- ✓ rock salt
- ✓ Epsom salts
- ✓ borax
- ✓ baking soda
- ✓ science notebook
- ✓ pencil

Granite and basalt are igneous rocks. Granite is the foundation of the continents and many huge mountain ranges, like the Sierra Nevada in California. The base of the ocean floor is basalt. Igneous rocks make up over half of the earth's crust.

The word *igneous* comes from the Latin word for "fiery." Igneous rocks begin deep in the earth where temperatures that reach 1,400°C (2,552°F) make rock flow like maple syrup. The liquid rock, called magma, is pushed to the surface through volcanoes as lava. This cools to form igneous volcanic rocks, like basalt and pumice. Other magma cools beneath the earth's surface and forms rocks like gabbro, diorite, and granite. Igneous rocks contain many minerals. The lighter-colored igneous rocks are made from the minerals quartz and feldspar. Darker igneous rocks contain mostly iron and magnesium.

The type of igneous rocks that form depends on the temperature and the available minerals. If the liquid rock cools quickly, it forms small crystals, like most volcanic rocks. Some are even like glass, with no detectable crystal structure. Magma that has cooled more slowly under the ground has time to form large crystals that you can see with your naked eye. This process forms such rocks as granite and gabbro.

HOW DOES THE RATE OF COOLING AFFECT THE SIZE OF CRYSTALS IN IGNEOUS ROCKS?

To make a crystal-forming (supersaturated) solution, **have an adult** slowly stir about ⅓ cup of powdered alum into ½ cup of boiled hot water in a glass jar until some solids settle to the bottom. **Wearing an oven mitt**, have the adult place half of the solution in a glass pie plate, and quickly place the plate in the freezer for half an hour. Place the remainder of the solution in another glass pie plate. Allow it to cool at room temperature. Using your naked eye or a magnifying glass, count (or estimate) the number of crystals in a 2.5-cm (1-in) square in each pan. Measure several crystals in each square. Record the information in your science notebook. Which pan has larger crystals? More crystals? Why would larger crystals form in solutions that cool more slowly?

Different igneous rocks are made from a variety of mineral crystals. To compare the sizes of different crystals from different solutions (or elements), **have an adult** make a supersaturated sugar solution by heating, not boiling, 2 cups of water in a pot on the stove. Slowly add sugar until some settles on the bottom of the pot. Follow the same procedure as you did with the alum solution. Did the larger crystals form under similar conditions? Does the rate of cooling affect the size of crystal formation?

Do different cooling rates have the same effect on different crystal solutions? Try rock salt (sodium chloride), Epsom salts (magnesium sulfate), borax (sodium borate), and baking soda (sodium bicarbonate).

Science Project Idea

People use igneous rocks for many purposes. Create a list of uses for different igneous rocks. Make a map (of your state, the country, or the world) that identifies where major deposits of these can be found. Why are some rocks common in some areas and not in others? Identify some of the processes used to prepare the different igneous rocks for human use.

Experiment 3.4

How Sedimentary Rocks Are Formed

Materials

✓ 1-gallon plastic milk jug

✓ scissors

✓ measuring cups

✓ water

✓ rubber gloves

✓ old spoon

✓ plaster of Paris

✓ pebbles and sand

✓ widemouthed jar

✓ 2 paper plates

✓ sealable plastic bag

✓ freezer

✓ clay soil

✓ dried grasses or straw

✓ crushed limestone

✓ gravel

✓ cement surface

✓ vinegar or lemon juice

✓ science notebook

✓ pencil

✓ rocks

✓ hammer

The Grand Canyon in Arizona is one of the world's most striking examples of sedimentary rocks. Made of sandstone and limestone, it is hundreds of millions of years old. The rich coal beds in Pennsylvania are also sedimentary rocks. *Sedimentary* means "settling." The most common rocks on the surface of the earth, including the surface of the ocean floor, are sedimentary.

Sedimentary rocks form in several ways. Physical weathering

(the forces of wind, ice, and water) breaks rocks into smaller pieces. These pieces will form a weak rock if they are forced together by pressure or held together by dissolved minerals. Shale and sandstone, the most common sedimentary rocks, form this way.

Some sedimentary rocks are formed when water rich in dissolved minerals evaporates. Gypsum, from which plaster of Paris is made, is a deposit left when water rich in calcium and sulfur evaporates. The salt you eat comes from halite, a deposit left when water with a lot of dissolved sodium chloride evaporates.

A third way sedimentary rocks can form is from the remains of living things. Some rocks (like coal) form from dead plant material under pressure for millions of years. Others (like chalk) form from tiny sea creature skeletons.

WHAT AFFECTS THE FORMATION OF SEDIMENTARY ROCKS?

Cut the top off a 1-gallon plastic milk jug, leaving the handle. Add 2 cups of water to the jug. Put on rubber gloves. Using an old spoon, mix 4 cups of plaster of Paris into the water. Never pour any plaster of Paris, wet or dry, down the sink. It will block the drain. Do any cleaning up outside.

Stir 2 cups of pebbles and sand into the plaster of Paris mixture. This represents the beginning of conglomerate rocks, a type of sedimentary rock that forms when rock fragments are glued together by another substance under certain

environmental conditions. Shape the mixture into eight 8-cm (3-in) rocks. Label a widemouthed jar as A, a paper plate as B, a sealable plastic bag as C, and another paper plate as D. In jar A place two rocks covered with water; place two rocks on the B paper plate; place two rocks in the C plastic bag and seal the bag; and place two rocks on the D paper plate (see Figure 10).

Figure 10.

To understand some of the ways that sedimentary rocks can form, place two rocks in a jar of water in the sun; two rocks on a paper plate in the sun; two rocks in a closed plastic bag in the sun; and two rocks on a paper plate in the freezer.

Place A, B, and C in the sun. Put D in the freezer. After two days, compare the four samples. In your science notebook, record the texture (hard, soft, disintegrated, etc.) and the appearance (cracked, solid, etc.) of each sample. What effect did the temperature and the amount of water or moisture have on the rock formation? What conditions must occur for the material in A to harden into a rock? Where might these different conditions occur in nature?

Make different sedimentary rocks by varying the type and amounts of materials used, such as clay soil, straw or dried grasses, crushed limestone, plaster of Paris, sands and gravels, and water. How do the drying temperature, the drying time, and the different components affect the strength of the rock? You can test the rock strength by **having an adult** strike it with a hammer or with another rock, or by dropping it onto a cement surface outside. How quickly can you "weather" or break down the rock? What happens if you add vinegar or lemon juice to the water in which you soak the rock? Where might this type of acidic rock be found in nature?

Science Project Ideas

⬥ Design an experiment to find out why evaporite (a type of sedimentary rock) develops in some areas and not in others. Create a map to show where major deposits of salt and gypsum, types of evaporites, are found. In what products is gypsum used?

⬥ Some rocks are made as the result of minerals falling or precipitating out of a solution. Design an experiment to show how stalactites and stalagmites form using string and two jars of supersaturated salt solution. Where are some famous deposits found? Why?

Experiment 3.5

How Metamorphic Rocks Are Formed

Materials

✓ **an adult**

✓ water

✓ pot

✓ stove

✓ measuring cup and spoons

✓ oven mitt

✓ glass jars

✓ shallow plate

✓ powdered alum (2.75 oz from grocery store)

✓ ruler

✓ labels

✓ marker

✓ thread

✓ 2 pencils

✓ waxed paper

Note: This experiment takes 4 to 6 weeks.

If the Leaning Tower of Pisa in Italy had been built on the same ground as the skyscrapers in New York City, it would not be leaning. The towering buildings of New York rest on a thick bed of strong metamorphic rocks called schists. Metamorphic rocks may also be pretty—emeralds, rubies, and diamonds are minerals found in metamorphic rocks.

Metamorphic comes from the Greek words *meta*, meaning "to change," and *morph*, meaning "form." Metamorphic rocks contain crystals that have changed form. It can be a small physical change, as when shale is pressed into slate and becomes a much stronger rock. Or it can be a huge chemical change in which crystals are actually rearranged. The stripes you can see in a schist rock occur because the crystals in the original rock were aligned in a new way as the new rock cooled. Metamorphic rocks are very hard, and many have wavy bands, stripes, or swirls where the crystals have reorganized.

If rocks form directly from molten liquid rock, they are igneous rocks. Metamorphic rocks form when rocks become solid under tremendous pressure or heat. There are three conditions that make the crystals in solid rocks change: heat, pressure, and available elements. Pressure and heat cause the crystals to move around, which changes the rock's physical structure. This is how limestone (a sedimentary rock) changes into marble (a metamorphic rock). If graphite, the stuff in your pencil, is subjected to tremendous heat and pressure, the carbon crystals rearrange into diamond, a metamorphic rock. The third factor is the presence of new elements. As the crystals are being rearranged by heat and pressure, new elements can work their way into the crystal structure, which is how rubies and emeralds form.

HOW DO CRYSTALS GROW AND CHANGE?

To make a crystal-forming (supersaturated) solution, **have an adult** boil water and add ½ cup of water to a glass jar. Slowly stir about ⅓ cup of powdered alum into the jar until some solids settle to the bottom. Pour 2 tablespoons of the solution onto a shallow plate and allow it sit for two days, or until you see two seed (small) crystals about 0.5 cm ($\frac{1}{8}$ to $\frac{1}{4}$ in) long. Save the remainder of the solution.

After the seed crystals have formed, **have an adult** make more crystal-forming (supersaturated) solution by slowly stirring about $\frac{1}{3}$ cup of alum into a glass jar containing $\frac{1}{2}$ cup of boiled water until some solids settle to the bottom. While the solution is still hot, stir in the remainder of the solution from which you made the seed crystals. Let it cool. Label two glass jars JAR #1 and JAR #2. Pour half of the *cooled* solution into Jar #1 and half into Jar #2. Carefully remove two small crystals from the plate and tie a piece of thread around each. Tie the other end of each string around 2 pencils. Suspend one crystal in Jar #1 (look back at Figure 9 on page 51). Keep the second crystal on a plate for later. Cover the jars with waxed paper. Let the suspended crystal grow for two to three weeks. Which jar is growing the bigger crystal? Which jar has only small crystals? Did the seed crystal in Jar #1 grow more quickly than any crystal in Jar #2? Why?

Have an adult slowly heat both jars in a pot of water on the stove. What happens to the crystals as the water temperature rises? Why do the smaller crystals dissolve first? **Have an adult** remove the jars from the heat using an oven mitt. Remove the suspended crystal from Jar #1, cover the jar in waxed paper, and allow the solution in Jar #1 to sit undisturbed for two weeks. Meanwhile, use the cooled solution in Jar #2 (the jar of small crystals) to grow a large crystal by suspending the second seed crystal from a thread into the jar. Why does a large crystal now grow in Jar #2? Can you cause the large crystal in Jar #2 to rearrange into small crystals again? Is there another factor besides heat that can cause a change in crystal size? (Hint: Think about pressure.)

Science Project Idea

In the creation of some metamorphic rocks, such as emeralds and rubies, new elements are added during the process of recrystallization. After you have grown an alum seed crystal, **have an adult** make a supersaturated solution of chromium sulfate (available from a science supply company). Let it cool and add it to the alum crystal solution. Observe the crystal changing color as it grows over two weeks. What happens if you add more chromium? What happens if you only add tap water, food coloring, or paint?

Experiment 3.6

The Rock Cycle

Materials

✓ **an adult**

✓ 8 graham crackers

✓ cookie sheet

✓ sugar cubes

✓ labels and marker

✓ oven

✓ oven mitt

✓ towel

✓ large rock (about the size of your hand)

✓ bowl

✓ spoon

✓ measuring cup

✓ peanut butter

✓ waxed paper

How is it that the calcium in the greens you ate, which is now in your teeth, may once have been in the teeth of a *T. rex* or in a stalactite in a cave in Kentucky? How is it that rivers continually carry sediment from the land to the oceans, but the ocean floor is still much thinner than the continents? How is it that rocks on the continents are billions of years old, but the ocean floor rocks are only about 200,000 years old?

The answer to all of these questions is because the earth is a huge recycling plant. Rocks and minerals are continuously recycled (see Figure 11). The denser ocean plates plunge under the lighter continental plates, dumping all the rock and sediment beneath the earth's surface. Under the heat and pressure below, the rocks partially melt. They eventually get pushed to the surface as a volcano erupts or a mountain is formed. Over more time, the mountain wears down, and the sediment gets dumped again onto the ocean floor.

Along with other sediment, the calcium from a dinosaur's teeth may have been washed back into the ocean. Then the calcium could have been uplifted to become part of a rocky mountain. Eventually the rock could have been worn down into soil particles, absorbed by a plant, and eaten by you!

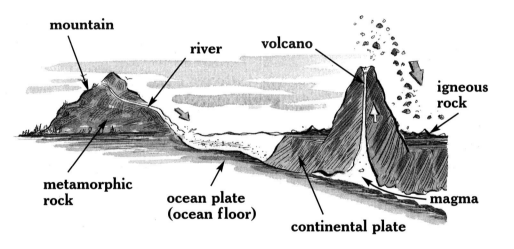

Figure 11.

THE ROCK CYCLE

The denser ocean plates plunge under the less dense continental plates. Ocean sediment partially melts under the surface. At some time, it gets pushed back to the surface through a volcano, during an earthquake, or during mountain building. Over time, the rocks erode and wash back to the ocean, settling on the ocean floor.

It is because of this continual recycling that rocks can be changed from sedimentary to igneous to metamorphic and back again. Remember, a sedimentary rock is a rock that forms from materials that have been deposited and cemented or pressed together. An igneous rock is formed when molten rock cools. A metamorphic rock is formed when any kind of rock is changed by heat or pressure.

HOW DOES NATURE RECYCLE ROCKS?

Break 8 graham crackers in half so that they are in squares. Place three squares on a cookie sheet, then cover each square with a layer of sugar cubes (see Figure 12). Add four more alternating layers of graham crackers and sugar cubes to each stack. The layers represent layers of different rocks. Label one stack as IGNEOUS ROCK and save it for your science project display to represent one stage in the rock cycle.

Have an adult put the remaining two stacks in an oven and cook them at 350°F for 15 minutes, or until the sugar cubes have melted. Using an oven mitt, **have the adult** remove the cookie sheet. Allow the stacks to cool. Save one stack for your display and label it METAMORPHIC ROCK: CREATED UNDER HEAT AND PRESSURE. This represents a possible stage in the rock cycle, when a rock is changed under heat and pressure.

To demonstrate another possible stage in the rock cycle, take the other stack from the cookie sheet and wrap it in a towel. Crush the stack with a large rock. Save half of the

"metamorphic rock"

"igneous rock"

"sedimentary rock"

"weathered rock pieces"

Figure 12.

To understand stages in the rock cycle, use layers of graham crackers covered with sugar cubes. Label one stack IGNEOUS ROCK. Bake the other two stacks. Label one of these METAMOR-PHIC ROCK. Break the other stack into pieces, and label half of the pile WEATHERED ROCK PIECES. Mix the other half with peanut butter and label that SEDIMENTARY ROCK.

crumbs for your display and label it WEATHERED ROCK PIECES. This represents the physical weathering of rocks.

To demonstrate another stage in the rock cycle, take the remaining crumbs ("rock pieces") and mix them in a bowl with ½ cup of peanut butter. On a small piece of waxed paper, flatten out the mixture. Label this CONCRETE SEDIMENTARY ROCK: CREATED WHEN MATERIAL CEMENTS ROCK PIECES TOGETHER.

In nature, how could rocks in different parts of the rock cycle change from metamorphic to sedimentary to igneous rocks? Start with each type of rock and trace a potential recycling route around the earth. Does the cycle have to occur in a certain order? Where does it end?

Experiment 3.7

Identifying Rocks

Materials

- ✓ **an adult**
- ✓ at least 5 rock samples
- ✓ white liquid correction fluid (sold with stationery)
- ✓ permanent marker
- ✓ magnifying glass
- ✓ towel
- ✓ hammer
- ✓ water
- ✓ field guide to rocks
- ✓ science notebook
- ✓ pencil

You have learned that rocks are made from one mineral or different groups of minerals packed together. The mineral combinations in a rock vary depending on the minerals available when the rock forms. Some rocks even contain organic material (material that at one time was living). Coal is a rock formed from prehistoric plants, and chalk is a rock made from microscopic pieces of shells.

HOW CAN YOU IDENTIFY ROCKS?

Although there are thousands of minerals on the planet, most common rocks are made from only a few. Many rocks can be identified using a magnifying glass to look at its general appearance, the minerals it contains, and their crystal size. Another clue is where you find the rock.

Collect at least five rock samples, and dab some white correction fluid on a small part of each. When it is dry, number the rocks from 1 to 5 with a permanent marker. Use a magnifying glass to study each of the five rock samples, and record your observations in your science notebook. Does the rock have certain patterns of colors, like the stripes found in gneiss, or definite layers? Does it show air bubble holes, as in tuff or basalt? Does the rock crumble easily, like a shale or sandstone? **Have an adult** wrap the rock in a towel and break a piece off with a hammer. Did the rock break along flat surfaces or did it crumble? What color is the rock when it is wet? Can you see different minerals in the rock, indicated by different colors? If you hold it in the light and turn it back and forth, can you see different crystal faces or flat surfaces, as you can with granite? Are there large crystals visible with your naked eye or are smaller ones visible only with a magnifying glass? Does it have a smell (shale might smell oily)? Is it heavy like granite or very light like tuff? Where did you find the sample?

Using the information you have observed, look in a field guide to identify your sample. Is the rock igneous, sedimentary, or metamorphic? Where was it formed? How might it change over time? What are the major rock groups in your state? Why are some rocks not found in your area?

Science Project Idea

Begin your own rock and mineral collection: collect, label, identify, and organize your rocks and minerals. Record the location and date that you find the rocks.

You can organize your collection in egg cartons or in a box with dividers. The way you group them can change as your collection grows. Possible groups are arranging minerals by hardness, color, specific gravity, or luster. What other ways can you think of to organize a rock and mineral collection?

Experiment 3.8

Different Soil Components

Materials

✓ 3 different types of soil samples (2 to 4 cups each)

✓ 3 large glass jars with lids

✓ labels

✓ marker

✓ water

✓ ruler

✓ science notebook

✓ pencil

If you pick up a handful of soil, how many states of matter are you holding? If you guessed all three—liquid, gas, and solid—you are right. The liquid part is the water held in the spaces between the solids in the soil. The gas is air, which is also found in those spaces. The solid components in soil are minerals and organic matter.

Organic matter is decomposing plants and animals and is dark brown. It takes up a small part of most soils, but it plays a huge role. As organic matter decomposes, it provides a constant supply of nutrients to living plants. It also slowly releases the water it holds to the plant roots. Organic matter causes soil to stick together in loose clumps, which creates more space for air and water.

The other solid component in soils is made from minerals. Mineral soil particles are only millimeters (mm) in size, and their size determines how they are classified—or what they are called. Sand is the largest particle (0.05–2 mm), feels "sandy" or gritty, and will not stick together when you press on it, even when it is wet. Silt is smaller in size (0.002–0.05 mm). Wet silt feels smooth when you rub it between your fingers, and dry silt feels powdery. Clay is the smallest particle (less than 0.002 mm). Wet clay easily rolls out into a ribbon (like a worm). When clay dries, it is hard-packed.

ARE THERE DIFFERENT SOLID COMPONENTS IN SOIL?

Collect three soil samples. Find soils that look and feel different (look near a stream or marsh, a sandy area, a deep hole, or a garden [or use potting soil]). Examine the three soil samples. Record your observations in your science notebook in a table like Table 5.

Details in a soil's general appearance can be such things as whether it has hard clumps, is wet and sticky, is full of tiny roots and leaves, or crumbles easily. For texture, rub the soil between your fingers. If the soil is dry, note whether it feels sandy, silky, gritty, or smooth like powder. If it is wet soil, note whether it feels silky, powdery, gritty, or both silky and gritty. For the ribbon test, note whether you can roll the wet soil into a worm shape. Does it crack as it dries? For the smell, note if it has an odor like rotten eggs or like a garden in the spring.

Table 5.

OBSERVATIONS: SOIL SAMPLES

	Color	General Appearance	Texture (wet)	Texture (dry)	Ribbon Test	Site Found	Smell
Jar #1							
Jar #2							
Jar #3							

Label three clear jars #1, #2, and #3. Fill each jar halfway with a different soil sample. Save a small sample of each for your project display. Add water to each jar to within 5 cm (2 in) of the top and shake thoroughly. Allow the contents to settle overnight.

Where did the heaviest particles settle? Organic matter is the dark material that is at the top or floating. Measure the height of each layer (see Figure 13). Estimate what percentage each layer is of the total soil sample. For example, if sand (light-colored material at the bottom) makes up 5 cm (2 in) out of the total 15-cm (6-in) soil column, it is 33 percent of the total ($^5/_{15} = 0.33$ or 33%).

Do the layers in the jars all look the same? Why not? Do all soils contain the same soil components? If you were to shake the jars again, do you think they would all settle at the same rates? Why or why not? Which soil samples do you think are mostly sand? Mostly silt? Mostly clay? Does it make sense to you that one soil would be high in a particular soil component (sand, silt, clay, or organic matter) and low in others?

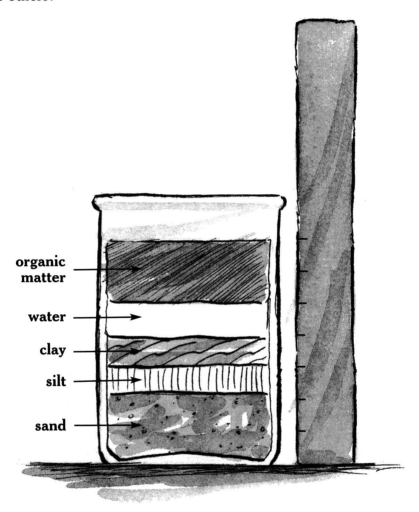

organic matter

water

clay

silt

sand

Figure 13.

To see the different mineral and organic components in soil, measure the height of each layer of soil in the jar.

Science Project Ideas

▽ Take one cup of each soil sample from Experiment 3.8 and put it in flowerpots labeled #1, #2, and #3. Plant 3 seeds in each pot. Keep the same light, water, and temperature schedule for each. Record the plant growth. Which plants grow the best? Compare plant growth to the soil information you collected above. Which soils are the best for the growth of this type of plant? Why? Can you give one soil type less water and still maintain good plant growth?

▽ Town and city planners, civil engineers, builders, and farmers all need to consider soil types because soils affect water quality and land use. Visit your city planning or zoning office to look at maps concerning soils, land use, and groundwater. Does your city have land use plans that consider soil types? Compare the groundwater maps and the zoning maps (or perhaps your city has groundwater overlay maps) to determine if the aquifer areas (groundwater deposits) and the recharge areas (land that drains water into the aquifers) are zoned for heavy industry or manufacturing. What resource (soils, groundwater, wetlands) protection measures does the city have in place? Are there cities that have stronger protection plans?

Experiment 3.9

How Water Moves Through Soil

Materials

✓ **an adult**

✓ 3 clear 1-liter plastic soda bottles

✓ screwdriver or scissors

✓ measuring cup

✓ 3 types of soil collected from different sites: a stream bank, a garden (or potting soil), a playground or sand pile

✓ ruler

✓ 3 small bowls or plates

✓ pans with wider base than bowls or plates

✓ water

✓ stopwatch or clock with a second hand

✓ science notebook

✓ pencil

After it rains, water can sit on top of the soil in a puddle, move into the soil, or flow away. The amount of water that goes into the soil is important for plants. Nutrients, substances that plants need to live, are dissolved in the water. If water moves too rapidly through soil, plants cannot absorb enough water or nutrients to grow well. And if water does not drain from the soil, many plants cannot grow.

Some soils do not absorb a lot of water, so the water just flows off the land. The water can remove the top layer of soil and deposit it somewhere else. The process is called erosion.

Soil particle size and its chemical makeup are key factors in how water moves through soil. Water moves quickly into and through soils that are very coarse, like sands and gravels. Water moves very slowly into and through soils that are fine-grained (like clays), packed down (like a walking path), or already wet. Some types of soils, like clay and organic soils, have charges (like a magnet) that hold water, and some, like sands, do not.

DOES WATER MOVE INTO AND THROUGH DIFFERENT SOILS AT THE SAME RATE?

Cut the tops from three 1-liter plastic soda bottles. **Ask an adult** to make several small holes in the bottom of each with a screwdriver or scissors. Collect about 3 cups of three types of soil from different sites: a stream bank, a garden (or potting soil), or a playground or sand pile. Rub some soil between your fingers. In your science notebook, record your general observations for each soil sample. For example, is it dark and smooth; light-colored and gritty; wet and mucky? Does it have a smell?

Fill one bottle with 20 cm (8 in) of one of the soil samples. Do the same thing for each of the other soil samples.

Take a bowl and turn it over on a flat pan. Place the bottles of soil on top of the inverted bowls (see Figure 14).

In your science notebook, make a table like Table 6. Be ready to record what happens, and the time at which it happens, as you add 1 cup of water to each soil sample.

Figure 14.

To understand that water moves at different rates through different types of soils, place the bottles of soil on top of inverted bowls. Add 1 cup of water to each sample and allow the samples to drain for at least 1 hour.

Table 6.

WATER MOVEMENT THROUGH SOILS

Time for Different Water Movement Events					
	Start first drip onto plate	Steady flow onto plate	Slow drip onto plate	Water stops dripping onto plate	General amount retained after 1 hour
Soil #1					
Soil #2					
Soil #3					

Allow the soils to drain for at least one hour. Measure the water that drained from the soil and calculate how much was retained in the soil. For example, if $^3/4$ cup of water drained from the soil, and you had added 1 cup, then the total amount held in the soil is $^1/4$ cup. Does water move through the soil samples in the same way? Where is the water that does not drain out? Is the time it takes for water to move through soil related to how much water the soil retains? To the size of the soil particles? Which soil might hold water long enough for plant use? Which soil might hold it too long and kill the plants? Did the water carry anything with it as it drained? How might a soil's ability to drain affect pollution traveling in soils?

Science Project Ideas

▽ Use the same experimental design as Experiment 3.9 to answer new questions. Does it matter if the soil is wet or dry to begin with? If you pack the soil down or freeze it first? If different soils are layered in the same bottle? If the soils are put in different orders in the bottles (clay on the top in one, clay on the bottom in another)? If you mix a hydrophilic (water-loving; like perlite) or a hydrophobic (water-fearing; like Styrofoam) material into the soil?

What happens if you dissolve a cup of salt in the water first? Let the water that drains evaporate and measure how much salt drained through. Is there any way to get the salt out of the soil? What happens if you mix oil or food coloring into the water first? Do some soils trap substances better than others (compare the water that you pour in with the water that drains out)?

▽ Go outside and look for areas in which water has moved soil—hills, fields, near storm drains, or muddy streams. Can you find places where water moves a lot of soil? No soil? Where does water collect after a rain? Can you find the place rainwater finally deposits its load? Could this cause any problems in the future?

Chapter 4

To Shape a Planet

The surface of the earth is always changing. Changes may appear suddenly, as in an earthquake or a flood, or they may take millions of years, as in the wearing down of a mountain or the drifting of a continent. Water, wind, ice, and other effects of the weather constantly reshape our planet.

There are two types of weathering: physical and chemical. Physical weathering breaks apart or wears down rocks into pebbles and soil. Water freezing and melting is an important physical process. Water expands by about 10 percent when it freezes. The action of water freezing, thawing, and refreezing in rocks causes the rocks to break apart. In a dry environment, heat can also cause rocks to crack. The outside of a rock heats and expands. As it cools and contracts, the rock undergoes more stress. Plant roots growing into cracks and burrowing animals also break apart rocks.

In the process of chemical weathering, rocks are worn down when their chemical composition is altered, forming new mineral content. Water is the key player in chemical weathering. Oxygen dissolved in water will cause iron in rocks to rust, or to oxidize. Carbon dioxide in water forms carbonic acid, a weak acid that can dissolve certain minerals. Plants also cause chemical weathering when their roots release acids that break down rocks.

Let's look at how water, wind, ice, and weather change the face of the planet.

Experiment 4.1

Rivers and Watersheds

Materials

- ✓ ruler
- ✓ large pizza pan or cookie sheet with rim
- ✓ aluminum foil
- ✓ large mixing bowl
- ✓ measuring cups
- ✓ flour
- ✓ water
- ✓ spray bottle with adjustable nozzle
- ✓ red, blue, and green food coloring
- ✓ label
- ✓ marker

After heavy rains, water levels in rivers and lakes rise. This is because rainwater flows down over the land into the lake. Water flows downhill for the same reason you roll down a hill—because of the force of gravity. But the shape of the land over which the water flows determines the downhill path it takes. When the shape of the land causes streams to run together, the streams form a river. Some rivers start high in snow-covered mountains and spend their lifetime moving water toward the ocean. The Mississippi River begins as a small stream in Minnesota and runs through ten states until it finally empties into the Gulf of Mexico in Louisiana.

A watershed is all of the land that drains water to a particular water body, like a river or lake. Watersheds are defined by the highest ridges of the surrounding land. A drop of water falling on a mountain ridge is going to fall into one watershed or another. Watershed boundaries are important because they determine what goes into an area's surface water and the groundwater. Watersheds affect not only the amount of water going into the lake or river, but also the sediment and even pollution carried by the water.

HOW DOES THE SHAPE OF THE LAND CREATE WATERSHEDS?

Place a ruler across the middle of a pizza pan, with one end extending past the edge of the pan by 5 cm (2 in). Crumple some aluminum foil (leave plenty of air spaces) to make a

15-cm- (6-in-) high mountain range across the ruler (see Figure 15). In a large mixing bowl, combine 8 cups of flour with 6 cups of water and spread it over the mountains and the rest of the pan. Make sure one side is spread evenly and flat. This will be the flat side, side A, like a prairie. Mix 2 cups of flour with 1 cup of water to make a thicker dough. Add this to the other side of the mountain to make a hill-and-valley side. Label this side B . This will be the valley side. Let it dry for an hour in the sun or until you see some cracks in the surface

Figure 15.

To see how water flows in watersheds, use dough to create a mountain that separates a flat area on one side and a valley and hills on the other side. Spray water down each side of the mountain.

of the flat side (do not let it dry completely because you want to reshape it later in the experiment).

Fill a spray bottle with red colored water. Spray side A of the mountaintop 15 times (do not let the spray go down the other side into the other watershed). What path does the water take? Record how far it travels. Spray 15 more times. What happens? Record the number of lakes and the number of streams that form. Refill the sprayer with blue water. Spray side B of the mountaintop with 15 sprays. How far does the water travel? What forms? Spray 15 more times. Record the number of lakes and rivers that form. Does the water travel down the sides A and B in the same way? Are the water bodies that are created the same? Why? How does the shape of the land affect how water drains?

Raise the ruler and watch how an uplifting of the earth's "crust" affects the two watersheds by observing the colored waters. Spray the new mountaintop (whatever is left) with green water and watch what happens. Where have new deserts, lakes, or deeper rivers been formed? Can you make lakes drain to form larger rivers? What else can you do to change the flow of the rivers? Where does the water running out of the watershed go?

Science Project Idea

Using the watershed design in Experiment 4.1, introduce some pollutants (use vegetable oil to simulate gasoline; pepper for pesticides; etc.) into different parts of the watershed. What can cause the contaminants to spread and to concentrate in certain areas? (Hint: Experiment with different weather events and crust movement.) What watershed protection plans are in place in your city? Find out by talking to your city planners or zoning officials.

Experiment 4.2

How Rivers Erode and Deposit Sediment

Materials

- ✓ heavy cardboard at least 30 × 92 cm (12 × 36 in)
- ✓ paved or packed surface (driveway or sidewalk)
- ✓ aluminum foil
- ✓ tape measure
- ✓ rice
- ✓ 2 types of soil (sand, garden soil, etc.)
- ✓ pebbles
- ✓ ½-gallon plastic bottle
- ✓ water
- ✓ watch
- ✓ science notebook
- ✓ pencil

Note: Do this experiment outdoors.

Flowing water in young, raging rivers wears away and transports huge amounts of sediment, rocks, and dissolved minerals. This process is called erosion. The force of the water and pounding rocks against the river channel makes the channel wider and deeper. Eventually it can carve out a valley or a canyon. Scientists believe it took 15 million years for the Colorado River to carve a mile-deep canyon through sandstone and limestone to form the Grand Canyon. Waterfalls are created when rivers plunge down over rocks that are resistant to erosion.

As a river gets older, the valley it carves gets wider. Older rivers can slow down, moving in wide S shapes called meanders. Sometimes these are cut off from the main river and become lakes. When rivers overflow their banks, they leave fertile floodplain soils behind. Many people are dependent on the food grown on these rich soils.

As rivers reach more level ground, the waters slow down and drop the soil and rock load. The deposits form fans or deltas. A fan forms where streams or rivers flow down from a mountain onto a flat valley below. A delta, such as the Mississippi Delta, forms where a river meets a large lake or an ocean that greatly slows its flow.

HOW DOES MOVING WATER TRANSPORT AND DEPOSIT SEDIMENT?

Fold a piece of heavy cardboard into a V shape that is 36 cm (14 in) high at its peak. Place it on a packed outdoor surface (driveway or sidewalk). Make a channel by folding a 30-cm (12-in) piece of aluminum foil in half. Fold the edges on the long side up so that there is a 5-cm (2-in) rim around it (see Figure 16a). Bend the top two inches of the foil to hook over the top of the cardboard (see Figure 16b). Fill the channel with one of three materials (rice, soil, or pebbles) at a time. For each material, pour ½ gallon of water down the channel in 15 seconds. These are heavy rain conditions. In a table like Table 7, record in your science notebook how far the water carries each type of sediment.

Table 7.

SEDIMENT EROSION BY RIVERS

Distance Sediment Was Transported		
	Light flow of ½ gallon in 2 minutes	Heavy flow of ½ gallon in 15 seconds
Rice		
Soil		
Pebbles		

a)

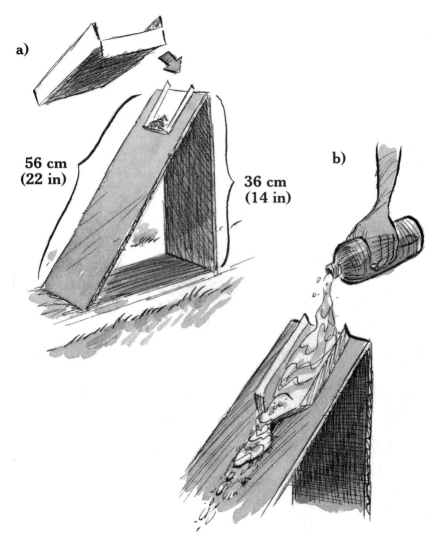

56 cm
(22 in)

36 cm
(14 in)

b)

Figure 16.

a) To observe the effect of water transporting different sediments, make a channel of aluminum foil and fold it over the top of the cardboard. b) Fill the aluminum-foil channel with different materials and pour water down the channel to simulate different rain events.

Repeat the procedure, but this time sprinkle ½ gallon of water over a two-minute period into the channel. These are light rain conditions. Record your results and make a bar graph of the data (see Figure 17). Does the rate of water flow affect how far sediment is carried? Is all sediment carried the same distance? What factors affect the distance sediment is carried?

What happens if you increase the amount of water being poured, but keep the time period the same? How does it affect the sediment travel distance if you decrease the slope of the channel by spreading out the cardboard? Do you think more

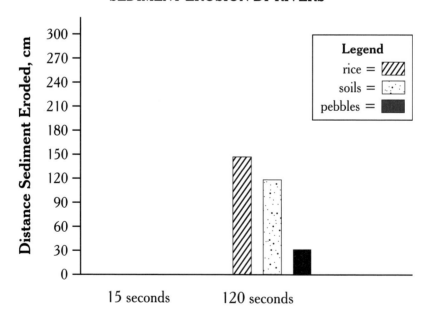

Figure 17.

soil is carried away in rivers that are steep and fast (younger rivers) or flatter and slower (older rivers)? What type of soil (heavy sands or lighter silts and clays) do you think reaches the end of a delta?

Science Project Idea

Using the experimental design from Experiment 4.2, construct a dam across the path of the water. How would a dam affect the wetlands downstream? Research the effect of dams on rivers and their floodplains and other wetlands. On the Internet, search: *river restoration projects in* [your state] or *dam restoration projects in* [your state]. Why are river restoration projects being implemented? How are state and local organizations involved?

Experiment 4.3

How Oceans Erode and Deposit Sediment

Materials

- ✓ black permanent marker
- ✓ plastic container about 15 cm (6 in) deep × 30 cm (12 in) × 20 cm (8 in)
- ✓ ruler
- ✓ sand or small aquarium gravel
- ✓ water
- ✓ small plastic toy piece (such as from Legos or Monopoly)
- ✓ 10 small stones (like gravel)
- ✓ 6 larger rocks (about ³/₄ in)
- ✓ spoon
- ✓ science notebook
- ✓ pencil

Almost all of the earth's water is in the oceans, which cover about 70 percent of the earth's surface. Coasts are where the land and the ocean meet, and they are always changing. Coasts in the southern United States have growing, sandy beaches and miles of salt marshes. The White Cliffs of Dover in England are made of soft chalk that erodes easily. Other coastlines are more stable, like the steep, granite cliffs of the Maine coast.

Shorelines are eroded by the power of moving waters and by the rocks and sand they carry. But, ocean water also transports and deposits sediment. The waves and currents move and sort the sediment. The sediments are deposited either on the shore (making beaches) or along the shore (making sandbars or islands parallel to the coast). Sediments from as far away as the New York coast have been deposited on beaches in North Carolina. Hurricanes can destroy an entire beach, but the next season more sands may be deposited in sandbars or islands parallel to the coast.

HOW DO OCEAN CURRENTS MOVE AND DEPOSIT SEDIMENT?

Using a black marker, divide the bottom of a plastic container into 9 rectangles. Fill the bottom with about 2.5 cm (1 in) of sand. Add 7.5 cm (3 in) of water to the container and stir the sand. Pour off the cloudy water. (Dump the water outside so that you do not clog your sink drain!) Keep adding clean water, stirring, and dumping out the water until the water you finally dump out is clear.

Pile all the sand so that it covers $\frac{1}{3}$ (or 3 squares) of the container bottom. Put a small plastic toy on the sand to represent a house. Scatter about 10 pebbles on the sand. Slowly add water until $\frac{1}{2}$ inch of water fills the side without sand (the sand should not be underwater).

In your science notebook, draw a box with 9 rectangles to represent the container as you see in Figure 19 (you will need 4 copies: 2 labeled WITHOUT JETTIES and 2 labeled WITH

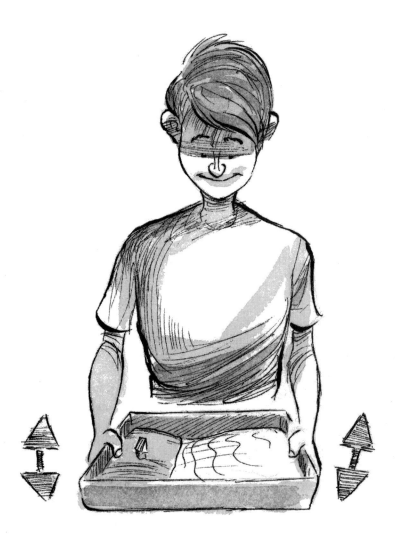

Figure 18.

To observe the effects of waves on beach erosion, pile 3 rectangles with sand. Fill the remainder of the container with water. Rock the container to simulate the different wave actions.

JETTIES). Sketch the sand distribution on the copy labeled WITHOUT JETTIES after each of the following events: (1) daily tide action: gently rock the container 10 times; and (2) severe storm: rock the container more intensely 10 times. Record your general observations in your science notebook. What happened to the pebbles? The house? The sand?

Set up the starting beach again (all sand piled in ⅓ of the container). Add a line of stones perpendicular to the line of sand to act as a jetty between the beach and the ocean. Add the water. Repeat the steps above and draw each new beach on the WITH JETTIES map. Record your general observations.

DAILY TIDE ACTION: WITHOUT JETTIES

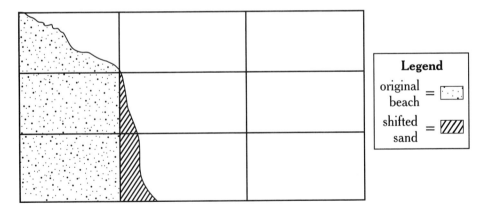

Figure 19.

Complete a chart for each tide event. This chart shows that the beach lost about ½ square of sand.

Using the data you have collected, make a table like Table 8. Calculate the percentage of sand lost for each of the events.

Table 8.

OCEAN EROSION AND DEPOSITION

	Without Jetty		With Jetty	
	Number of squares lost	**% Change**	**Number of squares lost**	**% Change**
Daily Tide Action	$^1/_2$ square	16.5 percent*		
Severe Storm	2 squares	66 percent*		
* each square = approximately 33 percent of the original beach, so $^1/_2$ square = $^1/_2 \times 33 = 16.5\%$; 2 squares = 66%				

Present the data from Table 8 (percent change) in a bar graph, like the one shown in Figure 20. How else could you present the data? How could you test how much surface sand shifts? How does the jetty change the sand erosion? Does it protect the house from washing away? Can you design other barriers to protect the beach?

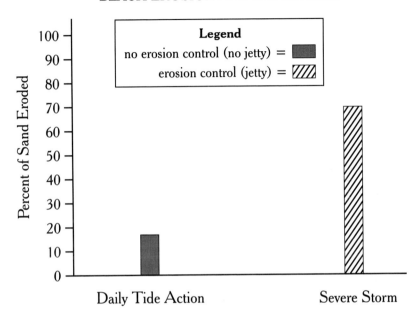

Figure 20.

Science Project Ideas

▽ Using the above experimental design, put colored sands and gravels offshore. Blow into straws to create different patterns of surface and underwater currents. Can you design a wave action that causes the beach to gain sand? To lose sand? Does it matter from which direction the waves are coming?

▽ There are over 400,000 kilometers (250,000 miles) of coastlines in the world. Create a map of the major ocean currents along the coastlines. What coastlines are losing sand and rock and what coastlines are gaining sand? What are the reasons?

Experiment 4.4

How Groundwater Moves

Materials

- ✓ marker
- ✓ plastic container about 15 cm (6 in) deep × 30 cm (12 in) × 20 cm (8 in)
- ✓ sand or small aquarium gravel
- ✓ water
- ✓ green and red food coloring
- ✓ measuring cup
- ✓ stopwatch, or clock or watch with a second hand
- ✓ 3-cm- (1-in-) square block (any material)
- ✓ vegetable oil
- ✓ sprayer from a spray bottle
- ✓ cheesecloth
- ✓ modeling clay
- ✓ gravel
- ✓ science notebook
- ✓ pencil

Do you know where your drinking water comes from? When you think of the earth's freshwater, you probably think of rivers, lakes, and reservoirs. But about 20 percent of our freshwater is underground. Groundwater can collect in large quantities and be stored in some geologic formations. Usually these are pockets of sands and gravels, but water can also be stored in rocks. Large deposits of groundwater are called aquifers. Drinking water wells can be drilled in these deposits. Some aquifers have held water for hundreds of thousands of years.

Just as with surface water, groundwater moves because of gravity. It does not move in underground rivers, but seeps down through the spaces between the soil particles or rocks. Water often moves from the surface into the ground. Under other conditions, water moves from the ground to the surface. For example, groundwater can break out of a hillside and form a spring. In this way, groundwater can supply water to wetlands (marshes, bogs, or swamps), rivers, and streams. Sometimes groundwater is moved by heat and pressure from below. For example, underground water near volcanoes can burst forth in hot springs and geysers.

DOES GROUNDWATER MOVE?

Label the opposite ends of a plastic container A and B. Fill the container two-thirds with sand. Mix in enough water so that there is a little water pooled on top of the sand (this means the sand is saturated, or all the spaces between the sand particles are filled with water). Now tilt the container and let any surface water drain out. Spread the sand evenly.

Dig a 5-cm (2-in) hole (or well) in one corner of the A end (see Figure 21). What happens?

Dig a 5-cm (2-in) hole (or well) in the opposite corner on the B end. Make a table like Table 9 in your science notebook. Time and record the following events:

Add ¼ cup green colored water to the B hole and record the time it takes for the green groundwater to reach the well at A.

well B

well A

Figure 21.

To see how groundwater moves, use sand and water. Mix in enough water so that the sand is saturated, and dig a well in each end. Add food coloring and tip the container to simulate different groundwater flow patterns.

Table 9.

GROUNDWATER TRAVEL TIME

Groundwater Travel Time, seconds	
Level well B to well A (green water)	
Well B to raised well A (red water)	
Raised well B to well A (red water)	
Raised well B to well A (oil)	

Place a 2.5-cm (1-in) block under side A. Now add red colored water to well B. Record how long it takes the red water to reach well A (or does it)? Lower side A and place the block under side B. Record how long it takes for the red water to reach well A. Now add ¼ cup of vegetable oil to hole B. Record how long it takes to reach well A. Do all substances travel at the same rate? Does an elevation change affect the rate of flow? Make a bar graph of your data (see Figure 22).

How could you stop a surface contaminant, such as gasoline or pesticides, from reaching the well? How about an underground contaminant, such as a leaking gas tank? What would happen to the flow if you pumped water (use a sprayer from a spray bottle with the bottom wrapped in

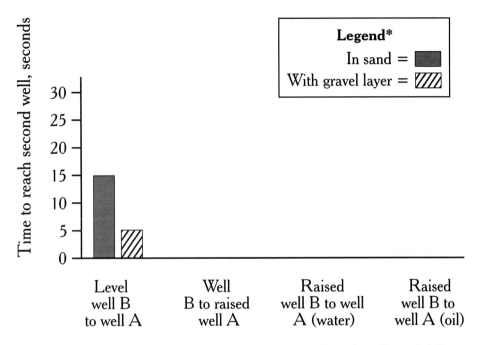

GROUNDWATER TRAVEL TIME

Time to reach second well, seconds

Legend*
In sand = ▨
With gravel layer = ▨

30
25
20
15
10
5
0

| Level well B to well A | Well B to raised well A | Raised well B to well A (water) | Raised well B to well A (oil) |

*You can add more bars to each well to show the effect of differer variables (gravel layer, nearby pumping station, clay barrier).

Figure 22.

several layers of cheesecloth) from a well between point A and point B? If you put a clay barrier at that point? A gravel layer? What other changes affect the rate or direction of groundwater flow?

Science Project Idea

Visit your United States Geological Survey, state geological survey, or city planning or public utilities offices to: 1) find out what your drinking water sources are; 2) look at maps of the land use and soil types around the drinking wells or drinking reservoirs and their watersheds or drainage areas; and, 3) discuss land use protection around those sites. Do an Internet search: *groundwater maps for* [your state] or *groundwater information for* [your state]. Make a model or a map of your city's drinking water sources, land uses, and protection measures. What are the protection issues for private drinking water wells?

Experiment 4.5

How Groundwater Erodes and Deposits Materials

Materials

✓ 1 rubber band
✓ 5 pieces of soft chalk
✓ rock (diameter about 10 cm, or 4 in)
✓ 1 box of sugar cubes
✓ 3 cake pans

✓ modeling clay
✓ pencil
✓ measuring cups
✓ hot water
✓ lemon juice
✓ water
✓ ruler

Water, no matter where it is, can create remarkable changes on the earth. You may know that the Colorado River carved out the Grand Canyon, but water works wonders under the ground too. Groundwater has formed over 580 kilometers (360 miles) of limestone caves in Mammoth Cave, Kentucky. Some of the caves have rooms over 36 meters (120 feet) high. Mammoth Cave is the largest cave in the world.

Groundwater does not rush and rage like a river, so how does it erode rock? When carbon dioxide dissolves in water, it forms a weak acid called carbonic acid. Most natural water contains some carbonic acid, so when groundwater comes into contact with rocks containing calcium (like limestone and dolomite), it dissolves some of the rock. The minerals get carried away, leaving caves or caverns. As groundwater continues to seep and drip through the limestone rocks, the water becomes saturated with calcium. The dissolved calcium precipitates out of the water in small layers as the mineral calcite. These small layers build from the ceiling like icicles and are called stalactites. Other drips accumulate on the floor, building stalagmites. Eventually they may meet in the middle to form columns. Many other minerals can be dissolved in the water, and these give many caves fantastic color patterns and crystal formations. Indeed, wherever water is, things move and change in remarkable ways.

HOW ARE UNDERGROUND CAVES CREATED?

Place a rubber band around five pieces of soft chalk (which is made of calcium, just like some rocks). Find a rock about the same size as the bundle of chalk. This represents rocks that are more resistant to being dissolved by water. Build a box of sugar cubes that is 6 cubes high, deep, and wide. Observing the sugar cubes will quickly give you an idea about how underground caves form over time. Place the chalk, the sugar cube box, and the rock in separate cake pans and cover them with a thin layer of modeling clay, which represents the ground surface. Only cover the top and the sides with the clay. With a pencil, poke five 1-cm- (^{1}/2-in-) diameter holes in the top of each clay covering (see Figure 23).

Figure 23.

To understand how groundwater can create caves, cover the top and sides of a bundle of chalk, a sugar cube box, and a rock in thin layers of clay. Poke five holes in the top of the clay and pour water into the holes.

Slowly pour 2 cups of hot tap water into the holes of each cave. Compare the effect of water on the sugar cubes, the chalk, and the rock. Over which "cave" does the land (clay) sink in places? Do caves form? Do underground lakes form? Does water have the same effect on each material? Now pour a mixture of lemon juice and water ($^1/4$ cup lemon juice in $^3/4$ cup of water) into the holes of each clay covering. This represents carbonic acid, a weak acid formed when carbon dioxide dissolves in water. Put your ear next to each one and listen. What do you hear? (The calcium carbonate should be "hissing" and dissolving.) Allow the chalk to sit in the water and lemon juice for several days. What conditions are necessary for underground caves and lakes to form? Will they form in all locations?

Experiment 4.6

How Wind Erodes and Deposits Sediment

Materials

- ✓ 6 sheets of newspaper
- ✓ measuring cup or scale
- ✓ small cardboard squares
- ✓ at least 3 different soils: sand; garden (potting) soil; dry, dusty soil (from a playground or dirt road); clay
- ✓ 5-cm (2-in) square of grass rooted in soil
- ✓ ruler
- ✓ small fan or hair dryer
- ✓ watch or clock with second hand
- ✓ water
- ✓ straw or grass clippings
- ✓ mesh fruit bag (like erosion netting) or cheesecloth
- ✓ grass seed
- ✓ small dish
- ✓ cotton or tissue squares
- ✓ science notebook
- ✓ pencil

Winds do not change the land surface nearly as much as the forces of running water and glaciers do. But winds have created white gypsum sand dunes that are so beautiful that the U.S. government designated them as the White Sands National Monument in New Mexico. On the other hand, winds can also ruin farmlands by blowing valuable agricultural soils thousands of miles, as it did in the 1930s to create the Dust Bowl.

Most winds cannot carry heavy materials like water can, but they can deposit materials over a much wider area. Winds erode soils from dry, unvegetated areas in two ways. Wind can lift lighter silt and clay into the air. The heavier sands move by bouncing along the land surface. A bouncing sand grain can dislodge another grain six times its size. As soils are blown away, huge hollows, or blowouts, form in the landscape. The process can also leave a surface of polished and pitted stones called desert pavement.

Eventually winds drop their load. There are two types of deposits, and these depend on the amount of wind, soil, and vegetation: mounds of sand are called dunes, and blankets of silt are called loesses. There are four basic shapes of sand dunes: longitudinal, parabolic, barchan (crescent-shaped), and transverse. Some dunes can move over 15 meters (50 feet) in a year.

DOES WIND ERODE ALL SOILS AT THE SAME RATE?

Spread six sheets of newspaper on the ground to form a rectangle. Measure (or weigh on a cardboard square) 1 cup each of at least three different soil types: sand, garden soil, playground soil, clay soil. Also include a 5-cm (2-in) square of grass rooted in soil. Place each soil sample on a cardboard square at the edge of the newspaper, about 20 cm (8 in) apart (see Figure 24).

Blow a fan or a hair dryer for three 15-second periods across the samples. Hold the dryer in front of the first soil sample and

Figure 24.

To observe the force of wind eroding soil, place different soils on a newspaper. Blow each pile for 15-second intervals with a fan or hair dryer. Keep the "wind" direction the same.

run it for 15 seconds. In your science notebook, use a table like Table 10 to record the distance the soil moved. Then run the dryer for 15 more seconds (for the 30-second reading) and record the distance. Run the dryer for another 15 seconds and record the distance the soil traveled (the 45-second reading). Make sure to point the fan in the same direction each time.

Table 10.

WIND EROSION DISTANCES FOR DIFFERENT SOILS

Distance Eroded in 15-Second Intervals									
	Most of the Soil			Farthest Any Soil Eroded			Total Soil Eroded		
	15	30	45	15	30	45	15	30	45
Sand									
Dry garden soil									
Clay									
Soil with grass									

To determine the amount of soil that eroded, subtract the amount of soil remaining (either in cups or grams) from the original measurement of the soil pile. If you started with a cup of soil, and ¼ cup remains, then $1 - \frac{1}{4} = \frac{3}{4}$ cup of soil eroded.

Make different graphs for each set of data (see Figure 25): (1) distance most of the soil eroded; (2) farthest any of the soil eroded; and (3) total soil eroded. Why does wind erode soils at different rates? How does the velocity of the wind (speed of the dryer or fan) affect the rate of erosion?

How would the same soil samples behave if they were wet or covered with straw, grass clippings, erosion netting (a mesh

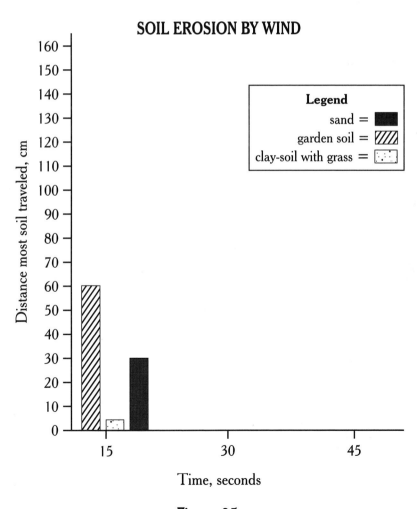

Figure 25.

bag), or new grass sprouts (plant seeds in the same soil)? Based on your data, what would you suggest as a best management practice (BMP) for preventing wind erosion of soil?

Where does the eroded soil go? Do the experiment again, but put a small dish of water on the newspaper (as a lake), and some cotton or tissue squares (as houses). What happens to the air quality? To the water quality?

Science Project Ideas

▽ Research the different shapes of sand dunes. Make a map of the world showing where those dunes are common. Using piles of sand, a small square of grass, and a hair dryer, create the four basic shapes of sand dunes: longitudinal, parabolic, barchan, and transverse. What causes different types of dunes to form? Why do scientists study sand dunes?

▽ Contact your local NRCS (Natural Resources Conservation Service) or city zoning inspector's office and find out about erosion control projects near you. **With an adult**, visit the sites to observe what they are doing and consider the reasons. Are there sand and gravel pits in your area? Are there regulations to control wind erosion? Visit the site on a windy day. Research sand and gravel pit zoning regulations of other cities or parts of the country.

Glossary

aquifer—An underground area of soils (usually sands and gravels) that holds large amounts of water and transmits them to wells.

asthenosphere—The upper layer of the mantle; the more rigid lithosphere overlies the asthenosphere.

clay—The smallest (less than 0.002 mm in diameter) mineral particle found in soil.

continental drift—The movement of the continents through the ocean. The theory developed in the early 1900s to explain how the continents were once one large continent; it was later replaced by the theory of plate tectonics, which states that the ocean plates and the continental plates are moving over the mantle.

crust—The thin, solid outer layer of the earth.

crystal—An arrangement of atoms in a repeating pattern.

delta—An area where a stream or river meets another body of water and deposits sediments.

element—The smallest unit of a substance; 92 elements occur naturally.

floodplain—An area on either side of a stream or river that is covered with water only when the water overflows its banks.

groundwater—Water located underground in the saturated zone of soil or rock.

igneous rocks—Rocks formed when molten rocks cool and crystallize.

lava—Hot molten rock (magma) that reaches the land surface.

lithosphere—The rigid outer layer of the earth; it includes the crust and the upper mantle and is about 100 km (60 miles) thick.

magma—Hot liquid (molten) rock found below the earth's surface; at the earth's surface it is called lava.

mantle—The 2,900-km- (1,800-mile-) thick layer of the earth that lies beneath the crust.

metamorphic rocks—Rocks that change from their original form when crystals in them are exposed to high heat, high pressure, and sometimes other elements. The rocks change while they are still in a solid state.

mineral—A crystal that occurs naturally and has a unique, orderly chemical structure; thousands of minerals are found on the earth (for example, gold, diamonds, calcite, and quartz).

organic matter—Material made from decomposing plants and animals; it gives soil a dark brown color.

plate tectonics—The interaction of the large plates that make up the earth's surface. The theory of plate tectonics in the 1960s replaced the continental drift theory. It stated that the lithosphere is made from individual plates that move and collide in many ways, producing earthquakes, volcanoes, and mountains.

recrystallization—The process by which existing crystals are rearranged and re-formed, forming metamorphic rocks.

sand—A mineral component of soil.

saturated zone—An area of soils in which spaces are filled completely with water.

sedimentary rocks—Rocks formed from materials deposited and consolidated, including pieces of existing rocks cemented with something else (such as sandstone) or rocks made from organic materials (such as coal and chalk). Some sedimentary rocks are left after water evaporates (such as rock salt) or when minerals precipitate out of the water (such as stalagmites and stalactites).

sediments—Particles resulting from the weathering of rocks and soils, by both physical and chemical processes.

silt—A mineral component of soil, ranging in size from 0.002 to 0.05 mm in diameter, which is between clay and sand. Silt makes ideal agricultural soils.

stalactite—An icicle-like deposit in cave ceilings that forms when dripping water leaves calcium behind.

stalagmite—A column-like deposit that forms on the floor of a cave when calcium-rich water drips down.

stratified drift—Deposits of sands and gravels washed from a glacier and laid down in well-defined layers.

supersaturated—A solution in which no more salts (solids) can be dissolved.

variables—Factors that can be changed, or varied, in an experiment.

viscosity—The measure of a fluid's internal resistance to flow. Water flows easily, so it has a low viscosity or resistance. Molasses has a high viscosity or resistance to flow.

water table—The top layer of the saturated zone; the upper surface of the groundwater.

Appendix: Sources for Material

GEOLOGY/HYDROLOGY (WATER RESOURCE) MAPS:

- http://www.usgs.gov

  (go to groundwater or surface water links)

- offices of United States Geological Survey (USGS) or your state Geological Survey, Natural Resources Conservation Service; or city planning or zoning offices

IRON FILINGS, CHEMICALS FOR CRYSTALS:

Science Kit and Boreal Laboratories
777 E. Park Drive
P.O. Box 5003
Tonawanda, NY 14150
800-828-7777
http://www.sciencekit.com

Carolina Biological Supply Company
2700 York Road
Burlington, NC 27215-3398
800-334-5551
http://www.carolina.com

Note: Your science teacher may have chemicals you can use for crystal growing. Be certain to follow all safety precautions with regard to proper ventilation, contact with skin and eyes, and disposal of these chemicals.

PLASTER OF PARIS:

- art supply store

POWDERED ALUM; ROCK SALT; BORAX (LAUNDRY SOAP); EPSOM SALTS:

- grocery store

SALOL (PHENYL SALICYLATE):

- pharmacy

- science supply company (see sources for crystals)

TOPOGRAPHIC MAPS:

- Maps a la carte, Inc.
  73 Princeton Street, Suite 305
  North Chelmsford, MA 01863
  http://www.topozone.com

- sporting good stores

- a city planning or building inspector's office

Further Reading

Bourseillec, Philippe. *Volcanoes: Journey to the Crater's Edge*. New York: Henry N. Abrams, 2003.

Gallant, Roy A. *Plates: Restless Earth*. New York: Benchmark Books, 2003.

Grace, Catherine O'Neill. *Forces of Nature: The Awesome Power of Volcanoes, Earthquakes, and Tornadoes*. Washington, D.C.: National Geographic, 2004.

Patent, Dorothy Hinshaw. *Shaping the Earth*. New York: Clarion Books, 2000.

Internet Addresses

Crystal Growing for Students
<http://www.xray.ncsu.edu/student_xtal.html>

United States Geological Survey
<http://www.usgs.gov>

USDA Soil Textural Triangle
<http://nesoil.com/properties/texture/sld005.htm>

Index